Celebrate with Song

...every parish can

Rev. Charles J. Matonti

Illustrations by John McAlinden

AVE MARIA PRESS
Notre Dame, Indiana

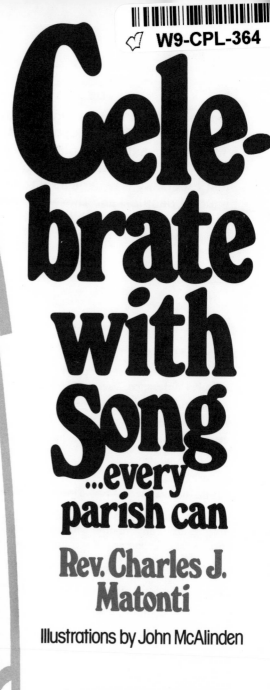

DEDICATION

This book about prayersong is lovingly dedicated to you and Bobby Baccigalupo and Mabel McGillicuddy and all the beautiful people with whom we have made—and will make—joyful noise unto the Lord. Most especially it is dedicated to two of those beautiful people—and these are their real names—Betty Breen and Charlie Matonti, my mother and father.

ACKNOWLEDGMENTS

Music in Catholic Worship, copyright © 1972, United States Catholic Conference. Used with permission.

Unless otherwise noted, scripture texts are taken from the *Good News Bible,* copyright © 1976, American Bible Society.

Portions of this book originally appeared as articles in *The Brooklyn Tablet.*

International Standard Book Number: 0-87793-245-X

Library of Congress Catalog Card Number: 81-71237

Printed and bound in the United States of America

Cover and Text design: Carol A. Robak

Text Illustrations: John McAlinden

Contents

Foreword

Charles Matonti asked me to read the manuscript of his book. If I liked it, he asked, would I write a foreword? I read it. I liked it. And here I am writing a foreword. And delighted to do it.

It goes something like this, maybe. I tease you, cajole you into reading Charlie's delightfully humorous interpretation of *Music in Catholic Worship,* the document by the Bishops' Committee on the Liturgy. (That is, if anybody reads forewords, ever. I reckon some do.) Then Charlie gets to tease you into reading the text itself. Then you get to discover, on your own, all the wonderful goodies that help you make beautiful life-giving celebrations of Sunday Mass. A sort of Rube Goldberg approach (and that dates me). But it works.

Father Matonti has the gifts of humor and of deep insight. These two gifts are not strangers to one another. In fact they belong together like the front and back of your hand. Louis Evely, I think, says that "humor is the nickname for wisdom." Charlie offers a fine show of this truth.

In chapter after chapter he helps us to look at "church stuff" as really not so different, not so far removed after all from the ordinary foibles and follies of everyday living. He helps us chuckle at them; not take ourselves too seriously. He helps us to laugh, not at, but with all the marvellous, lovable, everyday people who make up the parish Sunday Mass.

Precisely by means of his humor Father Charles helps us touch the deepest meaning and intent of the bishops' document on music in worship: Sunday Mass celebrations are most life-giving when people share themselves with one another.

Sacraments are not things. Sunday Mass is not a thing. Sacraments are the shared personal actions of all who celebrate. Faith, hope, love and healing are ignited from flesh to flesh, from person to person. The energy travels sidewise, horizontally. God comes to us through us. Jesus reaches us through the human signs we make.

Beautiful music, appropriate music, well-crafted music, honest music becomes in worship a powerful human sign through which people give themselves to people. It breaks down the barriers that keep people apart; it melts individuals into God's wonderful priestly people.

I helped write the first draft of *Music in Catholic Worship.* That is what we wanted most of all to say: Music is absolutely necessary for making life-giving celebrations. The many details that make up the bulk of the document make sense only in light of that very central principle: "Good celebrations foster and nourish faith. Poor celebrations weaken and destroy faith."

Father Matonti catches the message. So read his book and get infected and pass the infection on to others. And please laugh at his jokes.

REV. EUGENE A. WALSH, SS

What's happening in your church?

Are the people in your parish praying when they sing at eucharistic celebrations? Are they singing? Are they celebrating? Could you use some very practical suggestions, creative insights and helpful hints for liturgical prayer in your parish?

Would you like to read some funny stories about people experiencing musical prayer? And, speaking of reading, are you willing to read and reread the guidelines for contemporary liturgical music published by the United States Bishops' Committee on the Liturgy under the title, *Music in Catholic Worship?* For your convenience, the entire text is reprinted on pages 113–144. Are you willing to study the document, to discuss it, even to pray over it—and to continue the struggle to implement it more fully in your parish? It is not long and its further implementation might reasonably be considered a matter of life and death for our struggling parish liturgies.

That may sound slightly extravagant. And many priests and church musicians may nod (or shake!) wearily and say: "But what can another book or pamphlet or document tell us that we don't already know? We've tried everything. The people just don't like to sing."

I am reminded of a story about an old priest-friend of mine. Let's call him Rev. Howard Hugh Howard, S.T.D., Ph.D., J.C.D., pastor of St. Polycarp of Smyrna in a diocese not very far from your own. The time of this story was not too long after *The Constitution on the Sacred Liturgy* had been issued by the Second Vatican Council in December 1963. That document referred (in No. 112) to liturgical music not, as countless documents beforehand had done, as a "handmaid of the liturgy," but rather—and this was new—as a "necessary or integral part" of the liturgy. Father Howard's bishop commanded, therefore, that singing commence forthwith if not sooner at every Mass in all the parishes of his diocese.

Father Howard discussed this strange order with some of his priest-friends, found out what to do and spent most of Saturday doggedly typing a stencil.

He ran off the hymn-sheets before he went to bed and, the next morning, put them on a table in the back of his church. The sheets had the words for four hymns: "Praise to the Lord," "Lord, Accept the Gifts We Offer," "Humbly We Adore Thee" and "Now Thank We All Our God." And Father Howard Hugh Howard thanked God for helping him accomplish the task the bishop had given him.

He forgot, as a matter of fact, to mention the hymn-sheets from the pulpit. He honestly never even thought of trying to educate the people as to the nature of musical prayer, the why and how and what and when of liturgical music. But the hymn-sheets *were* piled on a table in the back of his church. Some people read them and wondered what they were for. A few people even took them home.

The bishop met the pastor a few weeks later at a confirmation. He smiled at Father Howard Hugh, poked him with his elbow and asked, "How's the singing coming at St. Polycarp's, Howie?"

The pastor shook his head sadly and said, "Well, we did all we could, Bishop, but I guess our people just don't want to sing. After a while, we had to give up."

Many priests and church musicians have grown weary in these challenging years after the Second Vatican Council. After some initial fears and hopes, excitement, achievement and frustration, some have given up—many years ago or only yesterday. Some, remarkably, have had success. (This phenomenon of success has occurred most often in parishes where concerned priests have hired competent musicians and persevered in planning liturgical celebrations with them.)

Music in Catholic Worship should continue to encourage us all, to revitalize men and women engaged in the process of continual renewal. Does the document really say anything new? Yes. How many of us priests, for example, were ever taught *this* when we went to the seminary:

> No other single factor affects the liturgy as much as the attitude, style, and bearing of the celebrant: his sincere faith and warmth as he welcomes the worshipping community; his human naturalness combined with dignity and seriousness as he breaks the Bread of Word and Eucharist.

That's Number 21 from *Music in Catholic Worship.* And that is certainly not just another way of putting what we have always said—even before Vatican II. That is a radically new insight and emphasis.

Any priest who is going to be the kind of celebrant described above, moreover, obviously has to begin before he gets to the altar. Planning is required. Team planning is required. That's still pretty new for a lot of churchmen. And it's not easy for those of us who were born and bred and even educated before collegiality was a word. Yet the priest is required to meet with the organist, leader of song, folk group, lector—whoever is involved in the liturgical action over which he is to preside. *Music in Catholic Worship* speaks of

> an organized "planning team" or committee which meets regularly to achieve creative and coordinated worship and a good use of the liturgical and musical options of a flexible liturgy (No. 10).

The document says again:

> The planning team or committee is headed by the

> priest (celebrant and homilist) for no congregation can experience the security of a unified celebration if that unity is not grasped by the one who presides, as well as by those who have special roles. It should include those with the knowledge and artistic skills needed in celebration—men and women trained in music, poetry, and art, and knowledge in current resources in these areas—men and women sensitive to the present-day thirst of so many for the riches of scripture, theology, and prayer. It is always good to include some members of the congregation who have not taken special roles in the celebrations so that honest evaluations can be made (No. 12).

The priest and other planners must take into consideration the "age level, cultural background, and level of faith" of the particular congregation for whom they are planning any particular liturgical celebration.

But how can this be done in St. Polycarp of Smyrna's? It's so idealistic. Can it be practical? Will the people on the parish liturgical committee be willing to meet with the celebrants to prepare more prayerful parish celebrations? Will the priests be willing to share preparation for parish prayer with their people? How would you handle it if you were Father Howard Hugh Howard?

Why do we do it?

There's only one way it can happen. And his name is Jesus. He is the way. People will be willing to prepare prayerful liturgies only if they have grasped the magnificent insights of the first few paragraphs of *Music in Catholic Worship.* That is the heart of the matter. It is all about Jesus and us.

This opening section of nine short paragraphs is entitled "Theology of Celebration," and it is vitally important. No part of the document is more important than this, its theological foundation. No one interested in contemporary liturgical music should even begin to wonder about what to sing and when to sing and how to sing, unless the wonder is warmed by a profound conviction about *why* we are singing. Priests and church musicians can profitably meditate on these first nine paragraphs of *Music in Catholic Worship.*

Consider, for example, the strength and simplicity of the first two sentences:

> A person is a Christian because through the Christian community he has met Jesus Christ, heard his word in invitation, and responded to him in faith. Christians gather at Mass that they may hear and express their faith again in this assembly and, by expressing it, renew and deepen it (No. 1).

Only if we believe that, can we work effectively toward creating more prayerful celebrations. The theological understanding of liturgy must be the foundation of practical questions about what and when to sing at Mass. Otherwise we may have "sounding brass and tinkling cymbals," but we will not have musical prayer; we will not have eucharistic celebration.

> The "Theology of Celebration" insists that we are celebrating when we involve ourselves meaningfully in the thoughts, words, songs, and gestures of the worshipping community—when everything we do is wholehearted and authentic for us—when we mean the words and want to do what is done (No. 3).

If we fail to celebrate well, moreover, we shall have not only poor celebrations but impoverished Christians.

> Faith grows when it is well expressed in celebration. Good celebrations foster and nourish faith. Poor celebrations weaken and destroy faith (No. 6).

Good celebrations require good music. And we do not have to search for the music of the spheres or the airs of angels to find it. It is not there anyway—not for us. We can praise God only in our own way. Human songs are sufficient for us. But

> they must be humanly attractive. They must be meaningful and appealing to the body of worshippers or they will fail to stir up faith and men will fail to worship the Father (No. 7).

In future chapters we shall consider practical applications of this theology of celebration. What is really *most* practical, however (and it cannot be said too often), is that we understand why we are working at liturgy.

> Christians gather at Mass that they may hear and express their faith again in this assembly and, by expressing it, renew and deepen it (No. 1).

If we don't start out (and keep going!) in that faith, there is little point to worrying about this or that communion song; there's no need to wonder whether or not to have a choir and what to do with it nowadays; there's no practicality in even the black and red hieroglyphics of music budgets or "How I Learned to Be Christian and Pay the Assistant Organist."

All of these questions do have answers which shall be explored in subsequent chapters. But they are simply dumb questions impossible to answer unless they are being asked by a believing Christian who knows what worship is all about. A priest, a church musician—anyone who is involved in contemporary liturgical music—must be *helping people pray.* That's first. That's really all.

The Spirit of Jesus within us sings praise to God, our Abba. It is in that faith and with that conviction—and only in that faith and with that conviction—that anyone can help God's people grow liturgically and, in the words of the ancient psalmist, "sing to the Lord a new song."

Some of God's friends are lousy singers

Clare McPhing isn't one of your everyday, run-of-the-mill non-singers. Even her best friends have told her, time and time again, that she has "bad voice." When she was a little girl singing to her Raggedy Ann doll, her mother asked her to shut up.

"Ah, Ma," Clare sobbed, "why can't I sing?"

Her mother answered with more sarcasm than sympathy, "I don't know, Clare honey. You just can't."

The only one who ever said anything good

about Clare's voice, as a matter of fact, was her husband, Isidore. Izzy once said, "Golly, Clare, you sure sing loudly in the shower."

At least, she thought he said "loudly." Anyway, he said it only once, and that was on their honeymoon, 37 years ago.

It is no wonder, then, that all the poor Clares of the world sit tight-lipped in our churches today, thinking, "Why don't we just pray at Mass? Why do we have to sing? What dimension is music supposed to add to our liturgical prayer? Can music ever really be prayer for us?"

The Bishops' Committee on the Liturgy answers emphatically in *Music in Catholic Worship:*

> Among the many signs and symbols used by the Church to celebrate its faith, music is of preeminent importance. . . . Music should assist the assembled believers to express and share the gift of faith that is within them and to nourish and strengthen their interior commitment of faith (No. 23).

Is music necessary at Mass? The document says:

> The quality of joy and enthusiasm which music adds to community worship cannot be gained in any other way. It imparts a sense of unity to the congregation and sets the appropriate tone for a particular celebration (No. 23).

What dimension does music add to worship?

> Music, in addition to expressing texts, can also unveil a dimension of meaning and feeling, a communication of ideas and intuitions which words alone cannot yield. This dimension is integral to the human personality and to man's growth in faith. It cannot be ignored if the signs of worship are to speak to the whole person (No. 24).

Let me give a personal and practical example of a parish community praying in song. It was "Right to Life" Sunday some years ago. I was presiding at a eucharistic celebration at St. Thomas More Church in Breezy Point. I suggested that we might sing "Hear, O Lord" as a special prayer for those (with whom we believed we were one in Christ) who could not pray for themselves because they lacked the strength, the patience or even the wits to do so—the dying, the very aged, the mentally deficient, the unborn. We, their brothers and sisters in Jesus, would pray for them:

Hear, O Lord, the sound of my call.
Hear, O Lord, and have mercy.
My soul is longing for the glory of you.
Hear, O Lord, and answer me.

The song, then, was not only announced; it was announced as a prayer, and as a prayer for a specific intention. We prayed the song that Sunday morning with more prayerful enthusiasm and more vocal strength than ever before. Almost no one sat with arms folded saying, "I don't like that song," or "I won't sing," or "Oh, leave me alone and let me be quiet. This used to be the only quiet hour I had all week."

Even Clare McPhing began to sing—believing that not only God but even her brothers and sisters were pleased and encouraged by her musical prayer. Even Izzy didn't seem to mind. Though, to tell the truth, maybe he couldn't hear her because he was praying with so much gusto himself.

We all sang because we accepted the privilege and the responsibility of praying, of being a priestly people. That is, after all, what musical prayer is all about.

Because that is what musical prayer is all about, however, it is obvious that not all music works as prayer for every congregation. If I had asked that same congregation (with the same appeal and for the same intention) to sing instead of "Hear, O Lord," say for example, Mozart's "Ave Verum" or the Beatles' "We All Live in a Yellow Submarine," we undoubtedly would not have had praying in that church that Sunday morning.

We might have had a little shocked silence, a little embarrassed laughter, a priest with a little egg on his face. We would not have had prayer.

How do we know what songs will make good prayers for a particular congregation? Judgments must be made. *Music in Catholic Worship* says, "To determine the value of a given musical element in a liturgical celebration, a threefold judgment must be made: musical, liturgical, and pastoral" (No. 25).

Competent musicians should make the musical judgment, bearing in mind that a variety of musical styles is encouraged in contemporary worship and that each song should be judged by the standards of its own style (be it medieval chant, folk ballad, Renaissance or contemporary polyphony, chorale or jazz).

In addition to this musical judgment, a liturgical judgment must be made, taking into consideration structural requirements and textual requirements as well as role differentiation. The planning team should ask whether a particular piece of music is appropriate as liturgical prayer and, if so, where in the liturgical celebration it should be performed and who should perform it: the celebrant, the entire congregation, the cantor, leader of song, the choir, the folk group, the organist or other instrumentalists.

Mozart's "Ave Verum" could be a magnificently prayerful communion meditation, for example, but only if sung by a well-rehearsed choir, not if sight-read by the average congregation at the eleven o'clock Mass at St. Polycarp of Smyrna's.

The Gloria from Bach's *Mass in B Minor,* on the other hand, would be unsuitable as musical prayer at that same Sunday Mass even if sung by the choir. The musical judgment is that it is magnificent. The liturgical judgment is that it is too big for the Glory to God at a parish Mass; it would take as long as the rest of the Mass put together—including Father Howard Hugh Howard's homily on simplicity.

Finally, in addition to being suited to the liturgy in general, the music must be suited to the particular celebration. The pastoral judgment looks at the people who are praying and asks whether this particular prayersong will help these particular people pray. What may be enormously helpful for a First Communion Mass might be slightly ridiculous at a Marriage Encounter Mass or a Mass of Episcopal Ordination.

What's the best way to find out which songs are most prayerful for most of the people at the eleven o'clock Sunday Mass at St. Thomas More, Breezy Point? That's easy. Just ask Clare and Izzy McPhing.

Sing to the Lord a new song—Please!

When I was a newly ordained priest, my pastor told me a wonderful story about a new pastor coming to the parish where he, Father Morgan Kelly, was a young curate himself. I may have some of the details wrong after all these years, but the story, which I have told often, is still a delight.

The story begins the day the new pastor took up residence in his new rectory and almost went out of his mind. What bothered the poor priest was this: For some reason, every time someone rang the rectory doorbell, a gigantic gong—like something at the start of a J. Arthur Rank movie—reverberated throughout the building.

This happened many times during the new pastor's first day and even a few times during his first night. He found himself sitting upright in bed in the dead of the night, screaming silently and clinging to the bedclothes for some comfort and support.

He didn't want to risk a coronary from the continual shock of the gong. So, the next day, he gathered his curates together and asked them what the story was.

All the priests stared blankly at their new pastor and asked politely, "Why? Is anything wrong, Father?"

"Yes," he said. "That gong! Why can't we have a doorbell like everyone else? You know, something simple, something that just goes ding-a-ling or ding-dong."

The priests looked around at one another. Then they looked at him again. Then they muttered one of man- and womankind's most ancient responses, "But we've always had that."

"Sure," the new pastor said between his teeth, "but what I want to know is why."

The priests thought very deeply for a rather long while and finally one of them remembered. "Oh, that's right," he beamed, "we got that gong for Hazel."

"That's nice," the pastor smiled. "Who's Hazel?"

Another priest answered, smiling too, "Hazel was the old housekeeper we used to have. We put in that gong so that Hazel could answer the front door. Hazel was hard of hearing."

The deaf housekeeper, the new pastor discovered, had left the rectory eight years before.

The gong disappeared that day.

We all get used to things the way they are, even when the reason for introducing them no longer applies. Consider, for example, the way we accepted Mass in Latin, long after the original reasons for keeping the Mass in Latin had ceased to exist.

The historical coincidence of three factors gave the Fathers of the Council of Trent sufficient reason to freeze the Mass in Latin. Faced with printing and vernacular languages, and with the Protestant reformers who had put the first two factors together, they were afraid that error might creep into the Mass itself, heresy into the holiest of sacraments. They froze the Mass to protect it and to protect us. They insisted that liturgy be unchanging in order to protect Christian worshippers from heresy.

Not many years after 1563, however, printing and vernacular languages were no longer associated merely with Protestants. The reasons for the Tridentine restrictions no longer existed even in 1600. Nevertheless, the restrictions themselves were in force until 1963.

Our liturgy was kept frozen for a full 400 years after the Council of Trent. The reason was gone, but no one thought to get rid of the gong. No one, that is, until Pope John XXIII gathered the bishops of the world together—in much the same way as the new pastor in Father Kelly's parish gathered his priests together—and wondered why.

Similarly, in 1958, a new Instruction on Sacred Music started most of us singing four vernacular hymns at Mass: entrance, offertory, communion and recessional. In 1958, those were the only four places in the Mass where vernacular songs were permitted. Entrance and recessional hymns could be considered occurring outside the sacred unchangeable Mass, since they actually took place before and after rather than during. Offertory and communion hymns accompanied revived ancient processions and did not interfere with the Latin prayers the priest prayed at Mass. These were the reasons for the gong of the four-hymn pattern.

The pattern became a syndrome. Today, years later, many of us are still singing in only those four places. The reason is gone but the gong remains. It is important, then, for us to know the historical background, to rethink the reasons today, to rid ourselves of unnecessary and distracting gongs.

As the Bishops' Committee on the Liturgy states in *Music in Catholic Worship:*

> Two patterns used to serve as foundation for the creating and planning of liturgy: One was "High Mass" with its five movements, sung Ordinary and fourfold sung Proper. The other was the four-hymn "Low Mass" format that grew out of the Instruction on Sacred Music of 1958. The four-hymn pattern developed in the context of a Latin Mass which could accommodate song in the vernacular only at certain points. It is now outdated and the Mass has more than a dozen parts that may be sung as well as numerous options for the celebrant (No. 52).

Music in Catholic Worship speaks, first of all, about sung acclamations as:

> shouts of joy which . . . are important because they make some of the most significant moments of the Mass (gospel, eucharistic prayer, Lord's Prayer) stand out (No. 53).

The document says further:

> In the eucharistic celebration there are five acclamations which ought to be sung even at Masses in which little else is sung: Alleluia; "Holy, Holy, Holy Lord"; Memorial Acclamation; Great Amen; Doxology to the Lord's Prayer (No. 54).

Today great variety is possible in the praying of these sung acclamations. They afford wonderful opportunities for combined use of choral and congregational singing. Even done simply, they can be quite strong and effective. But they must be done. Every parish, to speak most practically, has to start learning to sing a Holy, Holy, Holy sometime, sometime, sometime. We will not wake up some Sunday morning a dozen years from now and find that our people have learned a Sanctus by osmosis. They've got to be taught. And we've got to hire professional liturgical musicians to teach them. (For a humorous word of caution on this point, you might sneak a look at Chapter 17!)

Music in Catholic Worship speaks clearly about the liturgical significance of these acclamations and all other musical prayers of our eucharistic celebrations. The document should be read carefully by all priests, musicians, all parish planning teams concerned with the musical prayer of people today.

And all who read the document must notice that acclamations are placed first in importance. Next, two processional songs are described: the entrance and communion songs. Then, responsorial psalms.

Then, ordinary chants: Lord, Have Mercy; Glory to God; Lord's Prayer; and Lamb of God. Only then (and then only under the title "Supplementary Songs") does the document discuss the offertory song, a song after communion, the recessional song and the prayer of the faithful.

As should be obvious from even this brief outline, we have come a long way from the days of the four-hymn syndrome. But have we? Some of us, unfortunately, have not only not gotten rid of the gong yet, but we've just about gotten used to it. Nevertheless, the time has come for this gong too to be replaced. The directives demand replacement. Liturgical theology necessitates it. Our people need it if they are to sing to the Lord a new song which is meaningful musical prayer today.

Otherwise, we may find ourselves in the year 2358 singing the four hymns recommended in 1958, the way we found ourselves in 1963 with the Mass as frozen by the Council of Trent in 1563. It once took 400 years for us to remember—it really should take much less time for us to remember today—that all gongs must, occasionally, be removed and replaced with something which has a more contemporary ring.

Party time

Imagine yourself at a wonderful party celebrating your father's 75th birthday. The candles on his birthday cake have just been lit. Now, can you imagine yourself or your brother or your sister refusing to sing "Happy birthday, dear Daddy. Happy birthday to you!"?

Can you imagine your sister saying: "Oh, I really don't feel like singing right now. I'd rather just be quiet and stare at the candles. I'm really into candles"?

Can you imagine your brother folding his arms, shaking his head and groaning: "I don't like that song. Never did. Can't stand it, know what I mean? It's just not my kind of song and I'm not going to sing it"?

Imagine the same people in your parish church on Sunday. You are one with Jesus, eternal priest. You are filled with his Spirit. You have come to celebrate your life in Jesus to the eternal praise and pleasure of God the Father. Can you imagine yourself or your brother or your sister refusing to sing "Praise to the Lord"?

Carry the analogy further. Back to the birthday party. Each of the three of you—you, your brother and your sister—has a unique and special relationship to your father. He knows and loves each of you as an individual person. You, let us say, have a great sense of humor and you always make your father laugh, even when he's feeling sick or weary or lonely. Your sister's a great cook and is the only one in the world who can stuff and roast a chicken for him the way your mother used to. Your brother has a great voice and your father often (often after a couple of drinks) asks him to sing "Danny Boy."

But the moment when the candles are lit on your father's birthday cake is the wrong moment for you to ask your father if he's ever heard the one about the priest and the rabbi who met at the zoo; or for your sister to ask him what he'd like for dinner tomorrow; or for your brother to pipe up with "O Danny Boy, the pipes, the pipes. . . ." The old man is standing there, smiling a lot and crying a little, ready for the song celebrating this marvelous and important family occasion. He, reasonably, expects his children to sing "Happy Birthday" together and now.

In our relationships with God there are, similarly, times for private prayer and times for public worship. Every Christian must relate individually and personally to God. Unless we each do that, how can we all come together as a family with him? This coming together doesn't diminish our individuality; it presumes individuality, intelligence, good will, maturity, human vulnerability, sensitivity, courage and faith. We must have faith as individuals in order to express faith as a family—in order to grow in faith as individuals and as family.

These are not three strangers standing around the party table singing "Happy Birthday." A crowd of people has not just wandered in off the street wondering, "Whose birthday is it, anyway? Anybody know?" If each of these three—or three hundred or three thousand or three hundred thousand—persons did not know and love the father, and if the father did not know and love each of them, their song in common would be meaningless.

Worship demands faith and maturity. A child in a crib wants what he wants when he wants it. He simply screams his head off whenever he's hungry or wet or sore. We can't imagine an infant thinking, "I won't cry now. I'll wait half an hour or so and give my mother a little break. She looks rather haggard this evening." Infants don't think that way. It takes maturity to think of others. It takes maturity to unite with others in common cause. It takes Christian maturity to celebrate the Eucharist. It takes a family to sing the praises of God, our Father.

We are not at Mass to please our own tastes.

Mass is not some mystical museum where individuals pick and choose spiritual pleasures and treasures. We are at Mass to praise God together and to ask his help together. To do this, we need to be flexible enough to sing a lot of musical prayers which will not always please every one of us.

So the Bishops' Committee on the Liturgy says in *Music in Catholic Worship:*

> Flexibility reigns supreme. The musician with a sense of artistry and a deep knowledge of the rhythm of the liturgical action will be able to combine the many options into an effective whole. For the composer and performer alike there is an unprecedented challenge. He must enhance the liturgy with new creations of variety and richness and with those compositions from the time-honored treasury of liturgical music which can still serve today's celebrations (No. 76).

Parishes must have such musicians. They must hire them, encourage them, work and plan with them, and they must also pay them decent wages. The Bishops' Committee on the Liturgy says again:

> The Church in the United States needs the services of many qualified musicians as song leaders, organists, instrumentalists, cantors, choir directors, and composers. We have been blessed with many generous musicians who have given years of service even with meager financial compensation. In order that the art may grow and face the challenges of today and tomorrow every diocese and parish should establish policies for hiring and paying living wages to competent musicians. Full-time musicians employed by the Church ought to be on the same salary scale as teachers with similar qualifications and workloads (No. 77).

In the same vein of justice, the document warns:

> It is illegal and immoral to reproduce by any means either text or music of copyrighted materials without written permission of the copyright owner (No. 78).

More on this in Chapter 20, "How to Steal a Holy, Holy, Holy."

Good eucharistic celebrations in any parish, then, involve financial investments. It costs money to have qualified liturgical musicians. It costs money to have suitable and sufficient materials—sacramentaries, lectionaries and hymnals—for the celebrants, the lectors and leaders of song, the congregation and the choir. But every dollar spent on a good choir, for example, is worthwhile. The choir not only enriches liturgy with choral prayers, but it is today one of the most important and effective means of supporting and embellishing congregational song. More on this in Chapter 11, "Good Choir: A Necessity—Not a Lofty Ideal."

For a truly Christian community, is there any activity more deserving of our time, our energies and, yes, our money than our liturgical praise of God and our growth as his family?

A priestly people come together to praise the Father. At the moment when the candles are lit and the Father is there smiling at us, his children whom he loves, is there anything more important than our thanking him, loving him, singing his praises—and doing it well?

Pay the piper: clergy discounts

Did you hear about the priest in Oshkosh who figured out a way to save a fortune on the much needed redecoration of his church? He simply released within the walls of that sacred edifice crowds of crayon-carrying children and gangs of teenagers toting Magic Markers and cans of spray paint. Joke?

Did you hear about the priest in Kalamazoo who tried to save the total cost of repairing his school's broken boiler by doing the job himself with a rusty screwdriver and a blue ball point pen? Joke?

Did you hear about the priest in La Jolla who saved thousands of dollars a year on the liturgical music program for his parish by "hiring" Mabel McGillicuddy who used to play the piano a little when she was a kid (and who assured Father that she would be happy to be his parish organist and music director for nothing)? Father's choice had narrowed down to Mabel or some new guy in the parish who was married and had three children and a degree in liturgical music from Notre Dame and who was a fantastic organist and all-round music director (but who wanted a reasonable salary plus benefits and some job security, like a contract and all that). So the pastor decided on Mabel McGillicuddy for nothing. No joke.

With parish liturgical music, as with just about everything else in this world, we get what we pay for. It is possible to pay nothing. But then nothing is all we can realistically hope to receive in return. Nothing, that is, except maybe church walls done in subway-car messy-modern, school boilers that explode through the roof, and churches filled with people who cannot pray together in song.

Pastors who call in professionals when they have to, have to call in professionals now for liturgical music. They have to call in professionals now to help their priests and people pray together in eucharistic celebration.

It is understandable that, given our Tridentine training in liturgy and music, many priests felt incompetent and therefore insecure and uncomfortable when called to comprehend the needs of liturgy and liturgical music in the years following the Second Vatican Council. That is eminently understandable.

What is not understandable is the crazy system of priorities that prevents some priests from hiring professionals in this area—as they have had to do in so many other areas today. Is musical prayer not a high enough priority to deserve professional assistance?

Bishop Francis J. Mugavero of Brooklyn writes in his pastoral letter, *Of the Word, of the Spirit, Born:*

> All of us have felt the excitement, the exhilaration that accompanies those community celebrations where the music is carefully chosen, the people well-prepared and the musical leadership competent. We have to strive for this in every parish. This is not the place to skimp and save. Professional musicians should be employed and consistent and programmed instructions should be given to the people.

Do we really believe that? Today every pastor, priest and parish council member has to ask himself or herself questions like these in a contemporary examination of conscience:

- Do I really believe that liturgical music is not the place to skimp and save?
- Where is liturgy and liturgical music on my list of parish priorities?
- Is musical prayer as important to me and my parish as neatly painted church walls and nicely purring school boilers?
- Do I use a parish worship team that includes a paid professional music director?
- Does our parish council have an active liturgy committee? Do I listen to them and work with them?

- Do we ever ask the people what they think of the musical prayer in our parish, the songs we use, the instruments, the leadership, the participation materials?
- How much is good musical prayer worth to me and to my parish?

No kidding.

Experts are expert in making mistakes

"All the sounds of the earth are like music," Curly sang in *Oklahoma!*. Well, maybe sometimes they are. But they certainly weren't some years ago in Oklahoma City when members of diocesan liturgy commissions from all over the country met there for their annual convention. There were sounds of both harmony and dissonance in the convention score, and some cacophony as well.

Liturgical musicians, for example, were singing rather loudly and somewhat discordantly at publishers, and publishers were badmouthing musicians *con brio*.

Finally, with the cooperation of some publishers of liturgical music, the musicians proposed three resolutions:

> 1) That the Federation of Diocesan Liturgical Commissions implement copyright sharing by establishing a not-for-profit corporation which will research, collect, evaluate, refine, and edit a body of music for worship which shall then be made available at nominal cost to parishes, dioceses, individuals and publishers with easy accessibility and just recompense to composers and holders of copyright; 2) That the recommendation of this gathering be taken to the floor of the general assembly of this meeting that the music publishers of the United States be strongly urged to set up a clearing-house to facilitate the availability of their copyrighted materials to the parishes and dioceses of the country; 3) That the above-named processes be understood as initial steps toward the publication of a national service book incorporating the goals and ideals of our resolution at Detroit in 1972.

That particular solution to the very real problem of the accessibility of copyrighted liturgical music never did materialize. But much more dialogue at many more conventions, publishers' board rooms, chancery offices, choir lofts and church basements, over the years, has resulted in vastly improved understanding between most publishers and liturgical musicians. The harmony is not yet heavenly, but it's better than it was in Oklahoma.

Liturgists at that convention weren't spending as much time and energy fighting publishers as were the liturgical musicians. The liturgists had lots of other problems to discuss. How full a role should women play in liturgy? delegates at the Oklahoma convention wondered. How much forgiveness of sins can deacons give in their care of the sick? Shouldn't there be some clarification of ministries and orders in the church? Shouldn't new eucharistic prayers be prepared for children, for the deaf, for various people and occasions? Is there room for spontaneous prayer in eucharistic celebrations? And what about more training for bishops, priests and seminarians in liturgy and music? Finally, what about a national office of divine worship to help the bishops of our country effect liturgical development and growth and progress?

Resolutions were made and passed in all of the above areas and more. For the most part they were resolutions to urge action from the National Conference of Catholic Bishops. From the point of view of members of liturgical committees of parish councils, however, they are areas well worth thinking about and discussing. Priests and people in every parish still have to do a great deal of talking about parish liturgy and liturgical music. The talk will not remove all dissonance and tension from the air, but it will definitely help all the sounds of our liturgies to sound more and more like music. Honest differences of opinion are healthier than mutual apathy. In any parish, as in the convention in Oklahoma City, tension can be creative.

Two very different Jesuit priests who addressed the convention enkindled a great deal of creative tension. One priest was a conservative professor; the other was a circus clown. The professor urged priests to be total sacraments as parish priests; even their counting Sunday collections was priestly ministry, he insisted. The clown, a student of the art of drama and the communication of truth, insisted that all priests who celebrate Eucharist should be truthful signs—should mean what they pray and make clear what they are about as they are engaged with people and with God in liturgical celebration—or else they should not be allowed to preside! Both the professional clown and the conservative professor made people gasp and the air tingle with creative tension. Both provoked a great deal of thinking and rethinking and talking and sharing and hoping and planning for the future.

Do the members of the liturgical committee of your parish council ever get excited and involved in that kind of creative tension? Do we who are privileged to promote musical prayer give in too easily to discouragement and apathy? Are we afraid to take risks again, afraid to make more enemies, afraid to make more mistakes, afraid to "launch out into the deep" again as the Lord Jesus calls us to today?

In tennis, even the pros sometimes double-fault. Experts are experts at making mistakes. I have experienced the most unprayerful liturgies at liturgical conventions. After a week of seriously studying, analyzing and discussing liturgy and liturgical music, experts can put together a closing liturgy that discourages prayerful participation by its overambitious busyness, that ignores all the insights of the week's discussions, that infuriates rather than inspires. Some of the worst teachers I've ever had taught education courses.

So what are *we* afraid of? Harmony and dissonance can make such beautiful music together. All the sounds of the earth are like music after all.

Behold your Mother in songs from scripture

We Catholics have sung hymns to Mary in the recent past that might have been sung more appropriately to a thickly painted Hollywood starlet, vacantly smiling; or to a pretty pink pony on a Coney Island merry-go-round; or maybe even to a nice gushy cream puff. The songs were that poor—musically, liturgically and pastorally. As musical prayer they were beneath the dignity of the people of God and even further beneath the dignity of the woman pointed out to us in the pastoral letter of the American bishops, *Behold Your Mother—Woman of Faith.*

The bishops urge us to see Mary as she really is, as she lives and moves on and off the pages of the scriptures and in our lives today. If we really try to behold our Mother, and not just glance perfunctorily in her direction, whom do we see? Do we see a "lovely lady dressed in blue" floating around a million miles in the sky above us, who has no awareness of what hurts us and what helps us, who wants only "flowers of the rarest and flowers of the fairest"—flowers that grow in a world without fertilizer?

Or do we see a woman of faith and courage who believed when almost no one else believed, who said *yes* to God not only at the annunciation, but *yes* in the gaze of the questioning eyes of Joseph, *yes* in the stable at Bethlehem, *yes* during the flight into Egypt, *yes* when she did not understand Jesus when she finally found him in the Temple, *yes* to his *no* at Cana, *yes* again beneath his cross, *yes* at his tomb, *yes* waiting with the apostles at Pentecost?

Do we see Mary, not a million miles away, but Mother of the church, here with her children, a warrior-virgin who is not afraid to get her hands dirty helping us carry our crosses? Then what songs shall we sing to our Lady?

There are scriptural songs in her honor which both reflect her faith in God and give us an opportunity to imitate her faith in expressing and deepening our own. Lucien Deiss has written several strong and singable songs to Mary, songs like "Rejoice, O Virgin Mary" and "O Ever Radiant Virgin." Clarence

Rivers has written several contemporary songs in honor of Mary which he has used quite effectively in various workshops and liturgical celebrations.

When Father Rivers celebrated the Eucharist with our community at Cathedral College-Seminary, Douglaston, New York, some years ago, we worked out a Marian Mass together in which Father Rivers chose as his first reading—and it was a delightful surprise to hear it in church!—the wonderful story of David and Goliath! Mary not only bore a son of the lineage of David, she also had the disproportionate faith and courage and strength of David. That's the woman our songs should reflect and reveal and praise.

A great deal of variety is possible in singing prayers to Mary—without ever even approaching insipidity theologically or musically. At one Mass in honor of the Immaculate Conception, for example, we sang newly composed settings of both the Hail Mary and the Magnificat using antiphon and verses for congregation and choir. We also sang the medieval chant, "Salve Regina," the mid-19th-century "Sing of Mary" (which is simple and folklike but quite powerful when allowed to move martially), and one of our seniors sang Schubert's "Ave Maria" as a tenor solo with organ accompaniment.

Together we beheld our Mother—woman of faith, our patroness, our model of all that it means to be Christian today—and we sang our prayers united in faith like hers, like David's. We sang her sentiments in our Magnificat antiphon, "Our Hearts United Reveal the Lord and the Joy of God, Our Savior." Mary may not have had any "flowers of the rarest" that December 8, but she did have sons and daughters a lot stronger in their union with her and with Jesus and with one another—as men and women of faith. With Mary, our hearts united reveal the Lord and the joy of God, our Savior.

Wanted: not stars but leaders of song

Engelbert Humperdinck would probably make a lousy leader of song. So would Luciano Pavarotti. And Bruce Springsteen. And Liza Minnelli. Why? Because all of us in the congregation would naturally just sit back and listen to them sing. We'd never sing with them. They're all stars. They're not song leaders.

For leaders of song, we don't need stars. We need people who can carry a tune, certainly, but (and this is no less important) who can also carry a congregation. We need people who look as if they care whether or not we sing; who smile at us when we sing and work harder to get us to join in when we are not yet with the praying community. We need people who encourage us to sing—especially if all the members of our family have always put their fingers in their ears and groaned whenever we tried "Happy birthday, dear Gran'ma . . ."—even Gran'ma!

How does a congregation know whether or not its leader of song cares? There are signs. A good leader of song has done his or her homework; has gone over the songs with the organist beforehand; has decided on introductions and tempos; has decided which material needs rehearsal before the liturgical celebration begins. When introducing a song, a good leader makes sure that everyone has the song in hand before the singing starts. He or she leads with a good strong beat, not a fraction of a beat behind the instrumentalists but leading, keeping all together.

Most important, a good leader of song believes that we have gathered together in order to pray.

In addition to his or her role of leading and supporting the congregation in musical prayer, the leader of song may also function as cantor if someone else is not already fulfilling that role. As *Music in Catholic Worship* says of this liturgical role of cantor, "An individual singer can effectively lead the assembly, attractively proclaim the Word of God in the psalm sung between the readings and take his part in other responsorial singing" (No. 35). It is good for the cantor or leader of song to be responsible for the response to the first reading and for the gospel acclamation in any case, thereby leaving the scriptural readings in the hands of the lector as separate and special entities.

Any parish bright enough to employ leaders of song and/or cantors suddenly finds hundreds of prayersongs immediately accessible to the congregation with a minimal amount of rehearsal time. Responsorial singing is truly a godsend for our modern parishes. Many times, as in many of Lucien Deiss' musical prayers, the antiphon is short and strong enough rhythmically and melodically to be repeated instantly. And the cantor, choir or the leader of song can sing all the verses.

Thus the leader of song might not have to practice much with the congregation at all. The leader of song might just say, for example: "In our entrance song this morning, this last Sunday of Advent, we pray that Christ Jesus come more fully to us, to our families and friends, to all who need him, to all the world. We will sing, 'Maranatha! Come, O Christ the Lord!' The song is on Page 4 in the front of our service books. Please repeat the antiphon after me and I will sing the verses. Please rise now to greet our celebrant, Father Bob Baccigalupo."

The organist plays the antiphon once. The leader of song or cantor sings it once. The entire congregation then repeats the prayer, "Maranatha! Come, O Christ the Lord!"

The Lord comes quickly to such a praying community. And all of us singing come the more quickly to him. We've got faith. We've got vocal chords. All we need now to be Christian stars is leadership.

Let your fingers do the praying

There is a wonderful story told about Johann Sebastian Bach caught red-fingered and scarlet-shod at another organist's instrument. Bach, by the way, was reputedly able to play the pedals of the organ with his feet with more speed and agility than most organists could bring to bear upon the organ's keyboards with their fingers—or, for that matter, with their fingers and their feet put together! That is undoubtedly a slight exaggeration—as is the following story. But the story, like most legends, contains truth and, for many of our parish organists, I hope, encouragement as well.

Bach was walking in the country when he came upon a small, rustic church. He went in, prayed in silence for a while, walked over to the organ and, happily, found it unlocked. He sat down to play and pray—and did so brilliantly for over an hour, his fingers and his feet flying about skillfully, raising his mind and heart to God.

Meanwhile, the sounds of music reached the ears of the simple village organist who came running to the church and stood breathlessly at its doors with an enormous smile on his face and tears glistening in his eyes, his mind and heart at beautiful peace with God. When Bach stopped playing, or so the story goes, the other organist came timidly over to him and said, "Mein Herr, you are either an angel or Johann Sebastian Bach."

If I were making a movie of this legend, I would have Bach look up at the village organist at this point and say with the voice and the smile of Humphrey Bogart, "Well, I sure ain't no angel, Sweetheart!"

Because he wasn't. He was a dedicated Christian musician. Bach knew, as most every dedicated organist must know, the drudgery of repeated services; the demands of liturgical and musical perfection; the difficulty of raising one's mind and heart to God when one's mind and heart must necessarily be preoccupied with a complex multiplicity of liturgical and musical detail; the difficulty of remembering that attention to that detail is prayer, that music is prayer.

Bach knew, certainly, the thanklessness of his profession. Other professionals knew of his excellence, as did the village organist in the story, but the general public did not. Other organists were preferred for positions Bach wanted and deserved. Even more incredibly, after Bach's death priceless original manuscripts of his music were used to wrap fish and cheese in Leipzig. Leipzig then is not very far from Lackawanna now—or Lake Forest or Los Angeles.

For liturgical organists today the challenges are similar. For their vocation is to perfect their musical skills and understanding and artistry continuously, so that they may continue to help people pray while they themselves are praying. When the congregation is to sing, the organist must encourage, uplift and support its singing with proper introduction, tempo, volume, registration and musical variations.

But as the Bishops' Committee on the Liturgy has said:

> Singing is not the only kind of music suitable for liturgical celebration. Music performed on the organ and other instruments can stimulate feelings of joy and contemplation at appropriate times. This can be done effectively at the following points: an instrumental prelude, a soft background to a spoken psalm, at the preparation of the gifts in place of singing, during portions of the communion rite, and the recessional (No. 37).

In other words, liturgical music is prayer.

It is undoubtedly true that after the organist has helped people pray during his instrumental recessional, few members of the congregation will venture up the seven million steps to the choir loft to say thank you. That is even less likely than Bach doing an imitation of Bogart. And it is a great pity.

Nevertheless, the fact remains that the organist, who is undeniably neither Bach nor an angel, has helped people pray, has used music, the most profound of the arts, to help people do that which is most profound in their existence: to be touched by God and to touch God, to be with God, to pray.

And that, for both Johann Bach in Leipzig and Johanna Baccigalupo in Brooklyn, is glorious work.

Good choir: a necessity —not a lofty ideal

Does your parish have a choir? Is it good? Does it help you pray? Have you the voice, patience and generosity to join your parish choir, to pray with them and help others pray?

The Second Vatican Council in *The Constitution on the Sacred Liturgy* insisted that "choirs must be diligently promoted" (No. 114). The Bishops' Committee on the Liturgy in *Music in Catholic Worship* states, "A well-trained choir adds beauty and solemnity to the liturgy and also assists and encourages the singing of the congregation" (No. 36). Many church musicians maintain that a good choir is indispensable for the maintenance and development of prayerful parish liturgy today.

Why, then, do so few of our parishes have good choirs—or even mediocre choirs? Why were so many choirs disbanded in the mid-'60s, never to be resurrected?

The most obvious source of our present state of confusion is the Instruction on Sacred Music of 1958. This document set up a congregational four-hymn pattern which many parishes found difficult to grow into at first and difficult to grow out of subsequently.

As we saw in Chapter 4, it made sense in 1958 to sing four vernacular hymns at the only four places in the Mass at which it was then permissible to sing in the vernacular. It does not make sense today. There are many more, and many more important, places at which we can sing at Mass, at which we should sing at Mass.

Additional confusion was undoubtedly created in 1963 when the Second Vatican Council issued *The Constitution on the Sacred Liturgy* and insisted that "the whole body of the faithful . . . be able to contribute that active participation which is rightly theirs" (No. 114). Overcompensation was inevitable. Misunderstanding was understandable. Many tried to transform an absolutely silent congregation into an absolutely vocal congregation. Active participation was new. Active participation was now. Active participation was everything.

Where did that leave Sally Ann Soprano,

Adeline Alto, Tony Tenor and Bill Basso? For years they and other choir members had climbed faithfully up to the choir loft every Tuesday night after Miraculous Medal Novena to rehearse for next Sunday's eleven o'clock choir Mass at St. Polycarp of Smyrna's in Seattle or the South Bronx or San Antonio.

The stairs got longer and longer for Sally Ann, Adeline, Tony and Bill to climb until, one tragic Tuesday in the fall of 1966, Pastor Pancras Panicki pulled the steps up permanently and forever. Choirs were disbanded in the mid-'60s in parishes where the expanded and more comprehensive role of the choir was insufficiently or belatedly understood.

All the current teaching of the church on liturgical music insists that the role of the choir is fourfold: 1) the choir helps the congregation learn new songs; 2) the choir supports the congregation in unison singing; 3) the choir embellishes congregational singing; and 4) the choir sings music the congregation cannot manage, such as new verses of psalms or prayerful polyphonic motets in any language.

Music in Catholic Worship, quoting an earlier document of the Bishops' Committee on the Liturgy, describes the role of the choir today in this way:

> "At times the choir, within the congregation of the faithful and as part of it, will assume the role of leadership, while at other times it will retain its own distinctive ministry. This means that the choir will lead the people in sung prayer, by alternating or reinforcing the sacred song of the congregation, or by enhancing it with the addition of a musical elaboration. At other times in the course of liturgical celebra-

tion, the choir alone will sing works whose musical demands enlist and challenge its competence" (No. 36).

There is available today an ever increasing variety of settings for choir and congregation of many of the prayers of the Eucharist—prayers more important liturgically than an offertory hymn or a recessional hymn—prayers such as the Holy, Holy, Holy and the Great Amen. Choirs can help congregations pray these prayers.

At the same time, such prayers are a challenge and an accomplishment for choir members themselves. What self-respecting choir member would show up faithfully every Tuesday night at eight o'clock to rehearse "Now Thank We All Our God" which the choir will sing in unison with the congregation for the 437th time next Sunday at the eleven o'clock Mass? No wonder those stairs to the choir loft were getting longer for Bill and Addie and Tony and Sal.

They weren't learning anything. They weren't doing anything. They felt unnecessary. You can't build a successful operation with that kind of morale.

Moral: The church choirs which shall continue on into eternity are those church choirs whose members sing prayerfully and well—and help others sing prayerfully and well.

In any parish, choir members are a nucleus group of students of liturgical music. They are the only members of the parish congregation who come to rehearsals once or twice a week to study liturgical music. The necessarily brief practice sessions with a congregation before an actual liturgical celebration are certainly made smoother and more efficient by the strong support of a well-rehearsed choir to lean upon.

Consider the delightful feasibility of singing a new, musically excellent, prayerful hymn composed of antiphon and verses. The congregation repeats the antiphon after it has been sung by the choir. The choir can sing all the verses. This demands little preparation on the part of the congregation. If the people don't quite get the antiphon the first time, they will get it by the second or third repetition. Then, after the hymn has been sung this way for a few Sundays and the congregation is sure of it, it can be made even more beautiful by having the choir add harmonies above and below the melody line which the congregation is singing.

Then everybody smiles with surprise, suddenly finding himself or herself an instant member of the Mormon Tabernacle Choir. Choir members and congregation are pleased to be thus praying a beautiful musical prayer to God—and the only ones who have had to rehearse for more than a few minutes are the choir members! They are indeed a godsend and a treasure in any parish wise enough to encourage them and pray with them.

I can't sing when I'm crying

Gertrude McGillicuddy told me, "Confidentially, I'm afraid I might just choke to death singing Alleluias and all that newfangled stuff at funeral Masses."

Sister Miriam St. Polycarp of Smyrna told me: "It just doesn't seem right somehow. We all certainly believe in the resurrection but such a thoroughly joyful expression of that belief at the painful time of loss and mourning seems not only theologically strained and suspect, but psychologically inhuman and harmful."

Teresa Tebaldi told me: "I can't sing when I'm crying. Maybe Liza Minnelli can. But I can't."

Father Brian McLaughlin told me: "Jesus cried at the tomb of his friend, Lazarus. He didn't sing Alleluias."

I asked them all—Gertrude, Miriam, Teresa and Brian—to think about distinguishing between what is prayerfully possible and appropriate for the close family and friends of the deceased and what is possible for parishioners, neighbors, professional instrumentalists and singers gathered together with them at the Mass of Christian Burial.

I gave Gertrude, Miriam, Teresa and Brian a very personal and powerful example of that kind of distinction from my own experience at Cathedral College-Seminary at Douglaston, New York, where I had served as music director for many years. In our first six or seven years at Douglaston, we had more than our fair share of deaths and sang more than our fair share of Masses of Christian Burial: mothers and fathers (in their 40s, most of them) of our students, young brothers and sisters, priests on the faculty, Bishop Brian McEntegart, Monsignor John Fleming, our founding rector.

In fact, busloads of students and faculty were coming back to Cathedral after having sung a Mass of Christian Burial when we discovered that Monsignor Fleming had just been found dead in his room. Those were especially difficult days for all of us—as death not only touched us but walloped us around, over and over again.

And over and over again we got into busses and went to various parishes in the dioceses of Brooklyn, Rockville Centre and New York to sing Alleluias. Our choir, student body and faculty—some 300 voices strong and a powerful sounding prayer indeed—sang Masses of Christian Burial over and over again, welcomed in every case but two by the pastors, priests and parish organists.

In every case—and I believe that this is especially significant—in every single case, we received the most beautiful, moving, grateful letters from members of the family of the deceased. They invariably spoke about the way our faith supported their faith, the way our faith expressed in song supported their faith caught in pain and confusion. Yes, they believed in the resurrection. Yes, they believed that they would one day be reunited with their loved ones, never to be separated again. Yes, they believed, but that day of the actual funeral was a tough day for them.

They had very little energy left for Alleluias, for expressing anything but dazed hurt, shocked loss, desperate resignation. Our sung expressions of faith helped bring them up higher, closer to Jesus our risen Savior, present with us and within us. Our faith expressed in song helped family after family hang on in faith at a time when it was very difficult to believe, difficult because they hurt so very much.

It says a great deal for Christian communities, I think, that we can reach out to one another with this kind of support in faith; parishioners and other friends singing songs of faith express what those who mourn want to express but, at such a difficult time, cannot.

We, the living, support one another in our faith in the resurrection even as we pray for those who have died in the Lord. The Mass of Christian Burial is really about our living in and with this Lord, Jesus, here and hereafter.

I like to tell Gertrude McGillicuddy, Sister Miriam St. Polycarp of Smyrna, Teresa Tebaldi and Father Brian McLaughlin, and some other friends of mine as well, what one elderly priest said to me as we were unvesting after a Mass of Christian Burial recently. He said, "This new liturgy is certainly different from what we had years ago, isn't it? It's really about life."

Disposable music: a joy forever

For some strange reason, almighty and eternal God likes human and temporary music. It's probably for the same strange reason he likes us.

For all eternity, God the Father has been singing his Word, Jesus, embraced in their Holy Spirit. The song is somehow simply beautiful, filled with warmth and joy and love.

Today, wondrously, the Father sings this song within us, in the many churches of our world, as the

Spirit of Jesus within us sings "Abba . . . Daddy . . . Father . . ."—and sings it through the music of our struggling human instrumentality, through our voices good or bad, through our hymns magnificent or mediocre, modern or medieval, durable or disposable.

God has called us his children and has chosen in the mystery of his amazing love for us to need us to praise him freely, to bless him, to work at responding to his love and sharing it with one another. That work is crystallized in our liturgy.

And because we are human, all of our liturgical signs and expressions, including our liturgical music, must necessarily be human, and temporary. We shall never find the perfectly divine hymn which will last forever. Nor should we search for such a song.

Our search today is not for an answer, for a perfect and permanent liturgical music, for a new *Liber Usualis* to last another 400 years.

Our search and our need and our prayer today is for composers, choirs and congregations in the contemporary church to find many valid though varied answers. As Clement McNaspy has said in *The Renewal of the Liturgy* on page 185, "If the church is one and many, local and universal, divine and human, transcendent and immanent, eschatological and incarnational, it goes without saying that the forms of her worship will reflect this complexity, and so will her liturgical music."

If church musicians are ever to develop a healthy respect for this complexity and plurality, if they are ever to develop a sense of freedom in experimentation with contemporary styles of music for worship, they will have to be satisfied with a great deal of music that will prove effective but temporary.

Joe Wise, a good contemporary composer, has indicated, for example, that his "Take Our Bread" should be used by congregations only so long as it remains a means of prayer for them. It is not meant to last forever. It may get worn and dull with extensive use. It is effective prayer but temporary.

That is not a bad thing. Too long have church musicians scorned the temporary while they searched for the everlasting and settled for the archaic.

What we need now is a lot more new, fresh, disposable music sung for a while in all our churches if our prayers there are to remain alive. Disposable music, human and temporary, is indispensable for us today if we would continue to sing the praises of our almighty and eternal God.

Here comes the bride.... Not that song again!

Drums roll. A trumpet calls the guests to attention. A spotlight smiles on the entrance to the reception hall. A voice beams over the public-address system: "And now, ladies and gentlemen, for their very first dance ever, anywhere, as Mr. and Mrs. Brian Buonasera, our wonderful newlyweds have selected that beautiful ballad, "Something Stupid."

Would you believe "Strangers in the Night" or "You Don't Send Me Flowers" or "One Less Bell to Answer" or even "Colonel Bogey's March" from *The*

Bridge Over the River Kwai? Kwai not? After all, it's their party. They can cry—or laugh—if they want to. And the guests can smile.

It is the newlyweds' party, we all agree, and it should be their song—whatever that song is. And if they want to include all the 20th-century ritual of the reception hall with "Daddy's Little Girl," "Mr. Wonderful," the royal march of the flaming cherries jubilee, the traditional tossing of the bride's bouquet and the game-playing with the bride's garter—well, that too is theirs to decide. It is, after all, a party and it is theirs.

Does the same norm apply to the church ceremony beforehand? Can they have whatever music and other liturgical prayers they want there? It is their day. Certainly. But a party is a party—and a prayer is a prayer. Of course, they should help plan the wedding ceremony—including the music—but they must help their invited relatives and friends pray with them and for them. Songs and other prayers should be selected which will help all present participate in prayer.

We have all come not to observe a performance but to witness a sacrament—a sacred sign which gives hope to our love too—and to participate in prayer. The planners of the liturgy should help us do this. We have come, after all, not to a party in a reception hall but to a prayer meeting in a church.

The bride and groom, the parish priests, the parish organist, leaders of song, the parish folk group, or invited musicians who are friends of the family—all who are involved in planning the day's liturgy—should help make it the most beautiful prayer possible.

Personal, yes. Relevant, yes. Their own, yes. But more than that: the eternal prayer of Jesus for and with his bride, the church, here and now with this particular community, for this particular couple.

As the Bishops' Committee on the Liturgy has stated in *Music in Catholic Worship:*

> Great care should be taken, especially at marriages, that all the people are involved at the important moments of the celebration, that the same general principles of planning worship and judging music are employed as at other liturgies, and above all, that the liturgy is a prayer for all present, not a theatrical production (No. 82).

The general principles referred to above include team planning of the liturgy. They also include an evaluation of music in celebration which includes the threefold judgment discussed before: musical (is it good music?); liturgical (is it appropriate here at this place in the liturgy?); and pastoral (will it help this particular group of people pray?).

On that very last point, it must be remembered that circumstances can make a song prayerful for some which is a mystery or mundane (or both) for others. (More about this important understanding for liturgical music in the next chapter.) But suffice it to say now with regard to planning liturgical music for wedding ceremonies that everyone on the planning team (the bride and groom, the parish priests, the parish organist, leaders of song, the parish folk group, etc.) should be listened to with respect.

It can be a beautiful experience for a priest, for example, to hear a young couple explain how Paul Stookey's "Wedding Song" is a prayer for them and to read over the lyrics, "whenever two or more of you are gathered in my name, there is love, there is love. . . ."

I have been deeply moved as a man and enormously encouraged as a priest by young Catholic couples who prepare their nuptial Mass with enthusiasm and solid theological understanding, organizing the participation of their family and friends as lectors, servers, ministers of song, gift bearers, intercessors, eucharistic ministers in the eucharistic celebration of their wedding—even preparing their own participation booklet that all might celebrate their nuptial Mass beautifully and well. I find such young couples signs of great hope for me personally, sacraments of God's love and his continuing presence in his church. I love to listen to them.

The bride and groom and everyone on the planning team should be listened to with respect. Then a decision should be made together as to what will best help this particular congregation pray with and for this particular bride and groom. And that's not something stupid. That's something smart and sensible. It's so sensible, as a matter of fact, that it is the law of the church.

Impossible dream, possible prayer

Father Buonasera was very unhappy. The parish council was beating to death—over and over—the topic of secular song and sacred worship. Finally the priest asked in desperation, "What in the world has 'The Impossible Dream' got to do with our relationship with Jesus Christ?"

Joe Allegro answered, "It has everything to do with my relationship with Jesus Christ, Father." He went on to speak of a particular group of young people with whom he worked and celebrated the Eucharist, and for whom that song from the Broadway show *Man of La Mancha* was unquestionably a very real and precious prayer. His particular congregation, he explained, knew the show well and saw Don Quixote find treasure where others found only trash; when they saw him look at the cheap prostitute Aldonza and call her—and help her see herself as—the beautiful and lovely Dulcinea, they saw redemption.

Inescapably they saw Jesus and themselves. Especially when they sang the words, "And the world will be better for this, that one man scorned and covered with scars still strove with his last ounce of courage to reach the unreachable stars," they saw Jesus and themselves and, truly and profoundly, they prayed.

In our musical-liturgical-pastoral judgment that pastoral element is most important. For prayer is what we are about. But the pastoral judgment is also most difficult. For one man's prayer can be, if not another man's poison, frequently another man's distraction or boredom or headache or irritant.

Let's look at some examples. A friend of mine recently returned from England and was incredulous at having found congregations there singing the *"Tantum Ergo"* at Benediction to the tune of "O My Darling Clementine." Try it. If you're American, I bet you won't like it. It fits, but it doesn't pray—over here in the colonies anyway.

Someone who knew the old German love song from which our magnificently prayerful "O Sacred Head Surrounded" was taken might have similar problems. Some people also have difficulty praying hymns which call God "a bulwark never failing, protecting us with staff and rod"; other people consider that a powerful prayer indeed.

Basically the problem is one of moving out of a world of absolutes and into a world of plurality. Even in this new world it would be absolutely stupid to force "The Impossible Dream" on the highly varied crowd at the five o'clock Mass at the Church of the Good Shepherd in Holbrook next Saturday night. For most of them it would not be a prayer at all, but just some Broadway show song out of context. Plurality demands that we admit this. It also demands, however, that we admit that there can be a congregation for whom "The Impossible Dream" can be a prayer.

Today's liturgy demands that we know the people we are helping to pray and, in order to know them and help them, that we listen to them. We should ask the people in the pews what songs help them pray and what songs do not—and believe them—and help them pray. That is not an impossible dream either. It is what our liturgical laws call a required pastoral judgment.

Summertime, and the singing is easy

"Because it is so terribly hot out today," Father Vermeersch solemnly announced as soon as he had read the gospel, "we will cut out the sermon and the rest of the hymns at this Mass. Please stand for the creed."

Ms. Hazel Heinzel, the parish organist, blinked in disbelief. And two smart teen-agers by the back door mumbled to each other knowingly and simultaneously, "Cop-out."

For the church was air-conditioned!

Why didn't the people riot and demand a decent eucharistic celebration? One reason certainly was their attachment to virtues like reverence for the clergy and decorum in church. Another reason, just as certainly, however, was their lack of attachment to hymns and homilies.

A well-thought-out, well-prepared, tightly organized, relevant, lively, interesting, seven-minute homily would have been missed. But who could miss a rambling, disjointed, repetitious, 23-minute rehash of seminary ideas with little reference to the scriptures read that day and less reference to the people present? Not even Father Vermeersch.

A beautiful and powerful Sanctus praising the holiness and the majesty of God would have been missed. But who could miss singing a dragged-out "Humbly We Adore Thee" for the five-thousand-one-hundred-seventy-second time? Strong, bright, lively Amens and Alleluias involving congregation and choir would have been missed. But who could miss singing Ray Repp's "Allelu!" as if it were a dirge? Not even Ms. Hazel Heinzel, parish organist.

The work ahead of Catholic worshippers in summer is not air conditioning (necessarily), but education (necessarily!).

The work ahead of us in summer is not cutting out integral parts of the liturgy, but doing them well. Do we cut out the reception of communion because it is hot out? Then neither should we cut out the musical expression of our unity in Jesus—the communion song—because it is hot out. Do we cut out the Our Father or the Gloria or the words of consecration or the collections because of the heat?

Neither should we cut out a sung Sanctus or Memorial Acclamation or Great Amen for that reason.

There are many options available to adapt a given liturgy to given conditions—even atmospheric—but none of these options expects or allows us to leave out integral parts of eucharistic celebration. Many options could conceivably make a liturgy shorter; none should make it poorer, or, conceivably, incomplete.

Once, while I was on vacation in a diocese far from Brooklyn, I was startled by a strange request from a strange lady to do just that. I had been invited to celebrate the Eucharist at five o'clock one Saturday evening. I was vested and ready to start down the long aisle of the enormous, ugly, "all-purpose" building as soon as the leader of song and the organist began the processional hymn. Altar boys and lector were lined up with me.

Then, just as we were about to start down the aisle, the above-mentioned lady literally leapt out at me and said, "I hope they told you to cut out the sermon, Father? Hello."

I smiled and said (holding back some amazement and anger), "Don't worry, I'll try to make it a good talk. Hello."

She insisted, "We've got to set up tables for the dance here tonight and you're supposed to cut out the sermon."

"How about cutting out communion too?"

"Huh?"

"I'm not allowed to leave out the homily, but I promise I'll try to make it interesting and to the point."

"Oh?" I think she was almost as surprised as I was.

I really do not think that attacking a priest in the middle of his procession is what lay participation is supposed to be about. But it certainly says something about the kind of work—our liturgy—that looms before us all, even in summer!

As the patient said to the doctor, "Don't cut it out, just make it better"—even in summer!

How to keep people from singing in church

Let me warn you about all this singing at Mass. Whatever you do, don't let the people in your parish start singing those things called acclamations. No, those particular prayersongs are much too integrally involved in eucharistic celebration. The results can be devastating, as disastrous as something out of *The Sorcerer's Apprentice.* You may never get them to stop. Never.

A while ago we taught Father Ron Krisman's "Holy, Holy, Holy" to a normal group of people at a normal twelve o'clock Sunday Mass in a normal parish somewhere in the fairly normal Diocese of Brooklyn. The people's instructions were to sing the refrain, only the refrain: "Hosanna in the highest, hosanna in the highest." The leader of song was to sing the three verses: "Holy, holy, holy Lord . . .," "Heaven and earth . . .," and "Blessed is he who comes. . . ."

It worked beautifully the first week. As celebrant, I sang the people's refrain with them to encourage them to pray. I didn't sing any of the verses. "Let's all sing our refrain" was what my priestly bearing was trying to say.

I was trying to do the same thing the following week when suddenly I noticed something unbelievable happening. I was shocked. I didn't know what to do.

Marie Hennessy, a lovely 72-year-old grandmother in the 14th pew, was singing the first verse. She was supposed to be singing only the refrain. How could I stop her? Then Jack Baccigalupo joined her in the second verse. Then Harry and Jennifer Jackson and their three children. By the third verse, a dozen people were singing.

The next week it got even worse. Mabel McGillicuddy was singing the first verse as if she had written it herself. By the second verse, 60 people were singing. We had never taught them the verses. They were supposed to sing only the refrain. By the third verse a couple of ushers, Charlie Martinez and Frank Rogers, had come into the church proper from the rear vestibule (to discipline the unruly crowd, I hoped). But no. Even the ushers were singing. Believe me, this story is true. Only the names have been changed to protect the guilty.

Why is it that *Music in Catholic Worship* insists on the priority of acclamations over hymns in our eucharistic celebrations? Why do the United States bishops in these official guidelines for liturgical music in our parishes insist that the priority of prayersong be given to the gospel Alleluia verse; the Holy, Holy, Holy; the Memorial Acclamation; the Great Amen; and the Doxology to the Lord's Prayer? Did they ever guess where such legislation might lead us?

Once people were singing these acclamations, prayerfully highlighting the most important parts of the Mass, they started singing everything. People who had never before moved their lips to "Take Our Bread," "Be Not Afraid," "Immaculate Mary" or "Now Thank We All Our God" were now singing everything.

Once they started singing the prayers which they cherished as *their* prayers (prayers integral to the Mass they had always known), they discovered they could even sing hymns (those songs someone added to their Mass somewhere along the way). They knew that the acclamations were prayers of their Mass. They always had been. Once they learned to sing those prayers, they could sing the hymns as prayers as well. The people experienced liturgical music as prayer. Prayerful singing was part of their religious experience now.

Suddenly they weren't singing at Mass anymore. They were singing the Mass.

So, I warn you again: Whatever you do, don't encourage the singing of acclamations in your parish or the same thing might happen to you.

Folk groups are for praying

Father Jack B. Withitt, pastor of St. Pancras' Parish in Peoria, made a big concession to the times that were a-changing in the mid-60s: He let a few teenagers start a "folk Mass" at ten o'clock Sundays in the church basement. They were great kids: Peter Spentz, Polly Glaht and Mike Murray. They played guitar beautifully. They sang like professionals. And they really wanted to do this.

In fact, they had been hounding him every week

at Confraternity to do in their parish what was being done in almost all the neighboring parishes. A folk group playing and singing more relevant liturgical music, Father Withitt finally admitted, would attract back a lot of lost teen-agers.

It didn't.

People of all ages liked the music. Even the elderly recognized that there were more signs of life at the folk Mass than at the other "regular" Masses. The church basement had never seen more foot-tapping and smiling—except maybe at the St. Patrick's Day dance four years ago. But there didn't seem to be more singing at Mass, more active participation, more praying.

"Why?" Father Withitt wondered.

Everybody liked Peter Spentz, Polly Glaht and Mike Murray. Everybody liked the music. The harmony was gorgeous. And the kids were even writing their own songs. People loved to listen to them sing. After a while people started calling them Peter, Poll and Murray.

Ouch! And that was the problem. The folk Mass flopped because the folk group forgot what they were there for—or maybe they never really knew. They weren't there to be Peter, Paul and Mary. They were there to pray and to help other people pray.

Folk groups are for praying. They can't be all turned in on themselves like performing stars lost in the mystique of their music. The folk group's music is prayer. And its prayer is for all the people. What was said about the leader of song, in Chapter 9, is equally true of the folk group. The musicians have to look as though they want people to sing, as though they expect people to sing, as though they need people to sing. They are not only singers and instrumentalists; they are leaders of song, movers of musical prayer.

Peter, Poll and Murray never even looked at the people. So the people just looked at them—and listened. What was intended by Father Jack B. Withitt to stimulate new and increased congregational singing actually backfired into something like the old choir Mass at eleven o'clock upstairs where the choir sang musical prayers and everybody else just listened.

Sometimes that is a marvelous way to pray, listening to a choir or a folk group or a soloist. But not for the entire Mass. Why should we listen to three people singing the Lord's Prayer? It's the prayer of the entire family. We don't bring a trio of professional singers in to stand around our dining-room table all aglow with birthday cake and candles to sing "Happy birthday, dear Pop-Pop, happy birthday to you. . . ."

Folk groups are great, but liturgical music is our prayer. So much has changed, yet that has remained the same: Liturgical music is our prayer.

When I was first assigned to teach music in the seminary in September of 1963, every student owned his own *Liber Usualis,* our Mass was still perfectly Tridentine, our liturgical music was medieval chant, our liturgical language was Latin. There were rumors of possible changes someday.

On December 8, 1963, our patronal feast, the Second Vatican Council issued *The Constitution on the Sacred Liturgy.*

"There's a new world somewhere they call the promised land," we started to sing stammeringly. . . .

Prayerful song with guitar accompaniment was not welcomed warmly by all members of the seminary administration, faculty and student body. There was little vernacular music available. Prayerful lyrics were forced into sometimes strange fellowships with folk-song melodies. One of my favorites, which I wrote to the tune of—of all things—"Lemon Tree," went: "We are one, Oh my brothers. In Christ Jesus, we are one. His own Spirit lives within us. And his Father calls us son." If you could keep the lemon juice out of your eye, it could work rather well.

We have a great wealth of good, solid prayer-songs today, songs like Dan Schutte's beautiful "Before the Sun Burned Bright" and Bob Dufford's stirringly prayerful "Be Not Afraid."

We have songs for every possible use of instruments. How haunting it is to remember walking through the cloisters of the seminary on Palm Sunday at Douglaston singing Richard Proulx' processional hymn to the accompaniment of handbells—just handbells.

A wide variety of musical instrumentation and song styles can be liturgically blended in any eucharistic celebration. We can use a guitar at any Mass as a beautiful harplike background to the responsorial psalm, for example. Is there really any need anymore to speak of a "guitar Mass" or a "folk Mass"—or a "teen Mass"? Some of the best liturgical guitarists I know are adults, playing, singing and leading people of all ages in prayerful song at "regular" parish Masses.

Try this. It works beautifully. Let the lector at any Sunday Eucharist speak the response to the first reading. Have the people repeat it after the lector. Then, while the lector is praying the first verse of the psalm, have a guitarist gently pick the strings of the guitar. Notice how much more we all concentrate on the words of the prayer. The music focuses us better, opens us up more deeply, wakes us, moves us, touches us. We are praying. Music is helping us pray.

The same can be done with a flute, or a clarinet, or a muted trumpet, or a piano, or a harmonica or even the organ! *Music in Catholic Worship* (No. 37), quoting an earlier document of the National Conference of Catholic Bishops, and referring to *The Constitution on the Sacred Liturgy* (No. 120), says, "In the dioceses of the United States, 'musical instruments other than the organ may be used in liturgical services, provided they are played in a manner that is suitable to public worship.' "

It may be good therapy for seventeen young teen-agers to play the same strum, chung/chung/chung/chung, to accompany Bob Dufford's beautiful "Like a Shepherd," but it's awful musically, and almost impossible to pray with.

And prayer is the whole point. All instruments are sacred. All instruments can sing prayers. All instruments can make a "joyful noise unto the Lord."

The last psalm concludes:

Praise him with trumpets.
  Praise him with harps and lyres.

Praise him with drums and dancing.
  Praise him with harps and flutes.
Praise him with cymbals.
  Praise him with loud cymbals.
Praise the LORD, all living creatures!

Praise the LORD! (Ps 150: 3-6).

Music in Catholic Worship ends with this paragraph:

> We find today a vital interest in the Mass as prayer and here lies the principle of synthesis. When everyone with one accord strives to make the Mass a prayer, a sharing and celebration of Faith, then there will be unity—many styles of music, a broad choice of instruments, a wide variety of forms of celebration, but a single purpose: that men of faith may proclaim and share that faith in prayer and that Christ may grow among us (No. 84).

When Father Jack B. Withitt prayed that psalm and read that paragraph, a whole new world opened for him, a world he joyously shared with Peter, Poll and Murray and all the people of St. Pancras' Parish in Peoria. And all the people prayed and sang and lived happily ever after.

And to this day, whenever the wind is blowing in the right direction, you can hear the prayerful people of St. Pancras' Parish in Peoria saying, "Golly, how lucky we are that we've got Father Withitt!"

Cantate Domino canticum novum

Dear Abbe: As chairman of the music commission of the Diocese of Brooklyn, can you tell us if we are permitted to have our choir sing a good old Latin Mass anymore? I have enclosed details of what we're doing here.

Dear Good Old Latin: First of all, let me congratulate you and your choirmaster and organist and your priests and people. You should all be grateful and proud to have Sunday liturgies such as you outlined for me. I was impressed and delighted.

Secondly, let me answer the particulars of your question. You said that the congregation joins the choir in "the singing of the processional, the alleluia before the gospel, the response to the prayer of the faithful, the eucharistic acclamation, the concluding amen of the canon, the communion hymn and, most of the time, the recessional," and you asked whether or not, under these circumstances, it would be "compulsory at the sung Mass that the congregation join the choir in singing the Kyrie, Sanctus and Agnus Dei." In a word, no. You ask a legalistic question and legally the Mass program you have outlined is certainly acceptable for a particular celebration.

Liturgical vitality will, of course, demand more variety and a more creative use of options as you continue to pray together over the years. I am enclosing a copy of *Music in Catholic Worship* recently published by the Bishops' Committee on the Liturgy. You will see that the church's emphasis today is not on rubrics and legalities but on liturgical growth in Christ. Note the importance given the choir in Number 36 (which I have marked)—but note also that nothing is rigidly dictated as to what particular prayers the choir should or should not sing.

Nor is there any set formula for liturgical music anymore. There is no longer any such celebration as the "Sung Mass" or "High Mass" at which the traditional five movements (Kyrie, Gloria, Credo, Sanctus and Agnus Dei) were sung by the choir. Please note Number 52 in *Music in Catholic Worship.* Now, at any Mass, there can be any variety of prayers sung.

There is no reason why an occasional Agnus Dei

should not be done (even in Latin) by the choir alone. There is no reason why, for a particular celebration, the Glory to God in the Highest should not be done (even in Latin) by the choir alone. At the same time, however, a regular practice of retaining the traditional choral parts of the Tridentine Mass cannot possibly be reconciled with the current legislation and understanding of the role and function of contemporary liturgical music.

It is not compulsory that the congregation join the choir at every eucharistic celebration in singing the Lord Have Mercy, the Holy, Holy, Holy Lord, and the Lamb of God. But it would not be in accord with church teaching to create a parish formula for liturgy in which the congregation would always be excluded from these prayers.

You are obviously a dedicated and hard-working choir. Your long-range planning should aim at more variety in use of choir and congregation. Study the enclosed document carefully and you will understand what I mean. Or take this as an example (and please remember that it is only an example; it does not pretend to be a new, rigid formula):

- You might have the congregation sing a Great Amen which consists of only a few simple notes, which notes would then be repeated and embellished by the choir in magnificent polyphony.

- Then have the choir sing the first petition of the Lamb of God in unison. The congregation repeats it in unison. Then, for the third petition, the congregation sings in unison while the choir adds beautiful harmonies beneath and above and beyond the congregational melody line.

- Add a communion song in which the choir sings an antiphon in unison, the congregation repeats it in unison while the choir sings homophonically.

- As a meditation song after communion, the choir could sing a beautiful Renaissance motet (in Latin, of course).

A good choir is of vital importance to good liturgical music today. And a good choir cannot be maintained unless the members of the choir are given countless opportunities to be needed by the praying community of which they are an integral but special part. Choir members will obviously not continue coming to rehearsals to learn unison congregational songs. Nor should they be asked to do so. There is a vast repertoire of timelessly prayerful choral music for any choir to pray and master and pray again. The choir's role in contemporary liturgy is more important than it ever was, though it is in many respects different from what it had been for most of the 400 years from the Council of Trent to the Second Vatican Council.

If you consider the suggestions I made in the paragraph above (for the blended use of choir and congregation), you will see that the choir can easily and happily fulfill its important new role in contemporary liturgy. That role, as it has been emphasized in recent documents, consists in the choir's doing four things: helping the people learn and sing new songs; supporting the people in congregational singing; embellishing congregational song with choral harmonies; and singing prayers (such as meditation motets and other occasional songs) which are proper to the choir.

In conclusion, let me congratulate you once again on the liturgical prayer you have accomplished in the past. And let me assure you of my prayers and any other service I can give you that might encourage your continued growth as a praying community. I would make my prayer for you in the context of Number 23 from *Music in Catholic Worship*:

> Music should assist the assembled believers to express and share the gift of faith that is within them and to nourish and strengthen their interior commitment of faith. It should heighten the texts so that they speak more fully and more effectively. The quality of joy and enthusiasm which music adds to community worship cannot be gained in any other way. It imparts a sense of unity to the congregation and sets the appropriate tone for a particular celebration.

May your choir continue to assist your parish worship by adding that joy and enthusiasm and that all-important sense of unity in Jesus Christ.

Amen.

How to steal a Holy, Holy, Holy

Peter, Poll and Murray had another problem. Do you remember them? They were the ace folk group from St. Pancras' Parish in Peoria, people we met in Chapter 18. Their other problem was that after they had finally gotten all their musical prayer and role-understanding together, they discovered that they were professional musicians who had become professional thieves.

Father Jack B. Withitt was furious.

He read them the law. "Right here in Number 78 of *Music in Catholic Worship*," he told Peter, Poll and Murray, "it says,

> in order that composers and publishers receive just compensation for their work, those engaged in parish music programs and those responsible for budgets must often be reminded that it is illegal and immoral to reproduce by any means either text or music of copyrighted materials without written permission of the copyright owner. The fact that these duplicated materials are not for sale but for private use does not alter the legal or moral situation of the practice."

"But, Father Withitt," Poll remonstrated, "You've told us time and time again that we can't expect the people to join in singing a particular musical prayer unless they have the words in their hands."

"That's right, Father Withitt," Murray murmured, "you always used to get mad at us if we said, 'But, Father, everybody knows this one.' "

"Yes, Father Withitt," Peter piped in, "you'd say, 'Well, *I* don't know this one. There are too many similar words to remember. And I want to sing it with the people. How am I supposed to sing it if I don't have the words? Everybody has to have the words if we want everybody to sing, especially me. Honest, Father, that's what you said."

"Yes," Father Withitt rejoined, "I did say that. And I still say that. But I didn't mean we should steal. Golly, guys! Some wonderful composers have worked very hard to write these musical prayers. We shouldn't rip them off."

So together they investigated and found that some publishers had tried to make it convenient for them to use copyrighted materials. There wasn't yet a uniform policy. There was the pain-in-the-neck job of searching, writing and waiting for responses. But some publishers sold a license for a year to use any of their materials; others charged slight fees—or none at all—for permission to use their copyrighted materials.

Father and the folk group had the pain of some picky work ahead of them, but other people from St. Pancras' Parish in Peoria pitched in to help them. The work was finally done; permission was secured for all the materials they wanted to use. The charges were relatively inexpensive for all the good musical prayers they now had—legally and legitimately.

And, best of all, Father Jack B. Withitt, Peter, Poll and Murray, and all the people in St. Pancras' Parish in Peoria could now sleep in peace, their consciences at rest.

We went through a similar experience at the College-Seminary in Douglaston some years ago. No hymnal had all the materials we wanted and needed for our daily celebrations of the Eucharist—and World Library had discontinued the loose-leaf *Peoples Mass Book* which had been ideal for us to add our own materials to. So we did some more work, wrote for more permissions and created our own new book.

We were in for a rather strange surprise.

At the end of a year of working with our new hymnals, we collected them to store for the summer. Surprise! Shock! We discovered that half of them had been stolen—from chapel.

I had to position choir members as security policemen around the place with the half-facetious order, "Watch out for sisters with shopping bags and other alleged perpetrators with backpacks!"

Have you ever done that?—taken a book from a church, I mean. I have, I humbly admit. Examination of conscience time. You find a collection of songs that would be useful to you in your work. God certainly wants you to have it, doesn't he? Wasn't it God himself who providentially pointed it out to you? It's all God's property anyway, isn't it? We're all just one big happy family in the church, aren't we? They wouldn't miss just *one* book, would they? And it's for a good cause, isn't it? And, besides, everybody does it, don't they?

Not only do we defraud publishers and composers, we steal what is frequently stolen property back and forth from one another.

Kyrie eleison. Christe eleison. Kyrie eleison.

Didn't somebody once tell us that if we were coming to the altar to sing a song of praise to God and we remembered that the songbook in our hands was something we had stolen from our sister, we should stop and think and first go get permission from our sister to use her songbook and then come back to sing a song of praise to our God? Alleluia.

It was a story something like that, wasn't it?

Singing together in the Lord

Our liturgy is, quite simply, our life in Jesus. It is our life together as sisters and brothers of Jesus in our Father's family, the church. It is our expression or sign of this family life. It is also the way we grow together as Christians. Music is a major factor in this sign and this growth. Good liturgical music well performed is a beautiful human expression of our life together in Christ and an excellent means of expanding and deepening our life together in Christ. But what music? And where shall we use music in our eucharistic celebrations?

First of all, it must be admitted that every community is different. It is true that Christ is alive in every Christian community and that every Christian community is alive in Christ. But each community will have different musical abilities to express this Christian growth. There are, however, some suggestions which the Bishops' Committee on the Liturgy has made which are certainly applicable to every Christian assembly interested in intelligent, relevant, contemporary public worship.

The Place of Music in Eucharistic Celebration, a preliminary document to *Music in Catholic Worship,* surprised many readers with its statement about the four best places to sing at Mass. We might have imagined an insistence on the usual four hymns. But no. The document states that the four best places to sing are 1) the Holy, Holy, Holy; 2) the Amen at the conclusion of the eucharistic prayer; 3) at communion; and 4) in response to the first reading. We are advised that *other* places to sing are 1) at the entrance and dismissal; 2) the Lord, Have Mercy; 3) the Glory to God; 4) the Lord's Prayer; and 5) at the offertory.

Why this emphasis? You will have noticed that three of the four primary places recommended for song are part of the Liturgy of the Eucharist. The emphasis, then, is to insure that what is more important in eucharistic celebration is celebrated with more musical expression; and what is less important is celebrated with less.

If everything which can be sung is sung, this balance and proportion will probably be achieved in our act of communal worship. The danger is, of course, that "because any combination of sung and recited parts may be chosen" individual choice might make the Liturgy of the Word more musically expressive and impressive than the Liturgy of the Eucharist.

This would be so, to mention an extreme example, if we sang only the entrance song, Lord Have Mercy, Glory to God, responsorial psalm, gospel alleluia verse, creed and general intercessions. An unsung Liturgy of the Eucharist would seem pale in comparison.

The document states:

> The purpose of the service of the word is to proclaim the word of God in the Christian assembly in such a way that the people hear and respond to God's message of love and become involved in the great covenant of love and redemption.

The most important place at which the people sing during the Liturgy of the Word, then, is in meditative response to the scriptural reading. This is best sung by congregation, choir or cantor. If it is not sung, it is better that it be recited, not by the whole congregation, but by an individual, perhaps with unobtrusive organ accompaniment.

The purpose of music during the Liturgy of the Eucharist is to help the community live and love. And, as we have seen, the three places which are most important to emphasize in song during the Liturgy of the Eucharist are the Holy, Holy, Holy, the Great Amen and communion.

Amen is a small word, but it is most important—especially at the conclusion of the eucharistic prayer. It is then the yes which the people respond to the entire loving sacrifice of Christ and themselves.

> This great Amen will be much more meaningful and effective when sung. Among the most urgent tasks for composers is that of providing suitable settings for these acclamations. . . . It is difficult to make an enthusiastic acclamation out of this single two-syllable word. Composers should feel free to repeat it several times or to explicate its many meanings when setting it to music.

What must be emphasized by us at this point of the Mass—as throughout the eucharistic celebration—is intelligent musical artistry and deep Christian faith. We must know why we are singing this song now—and we must mean it. Liturgical music must be a good, human expression of our life together in Jesus and must be so appropriate to both the faith and the musical abilities of people, priest, cantors and choir as to deepen our life together in Jesus.

Now, more than ever, one who sings—and especially one who accompanies and directs communal singing in eucharistic celebration—prays twice. For as a whole human person, he or she rejoices in the heart of God the Father, and encourages in faith—and grows in love with—his or her brothers and sisters in Christ Jesus.

I'm sorry I can't sing "I'm sorry"

Reconciliation and forgiveness are essential elements of every eucharistic celebration.

God is great at reconciliation and forgiveness.

I'm not. Are you?

I'd love to hear Luciano Pavarotti sing "Amore, Scusami." I'd love to watch Linda Ronstadt sing "I'm Sorry." But I find it hard myself to sing, or even to say, "I'm sorry." Do you know what I mean? I mean for a lot of us human beings it's harder to say "I'm sorry" than it is to say "Fazi-battaglia verdicchio." Why? It's hard to say.

Marjorie Mertz, for example, told me: "Father, I was so angry at my husband, Mortimer, for what he said about my mother that I . . . well, I know this is awful, Father . . . but, well, I wouldn't even give him the kiss of peace at Mass on Sunday."

Sound familiar? But what can we do?

Music in Catholic Worship says:

> People in love make signs of love, not only to express their love but also to deepen it. Love never expressed dies. Christians' love for Christ and for each other, Christians' faith in Christ and in each other, must be expressed in the signs and symbols of celebration or it will die (No. 4).

Harvard Hupalowski told me: "Oh sure, Father, we all sing together at Mass—the whole family, I mean—and we all receive communion together and everything. But we don't go to the ten o'clock Mass anymore, Father, because my brother, Guy, lectors at the ten and we're not talking to each other, you see. Know what I mean, Father?"

Music in Catholic Worship says:

> We are celebrating when we involve ourselves meaningfully in the thoughts, words, songs, and gestures of the worshipping community—when everything we do is wholehearted and authentic for us—when we mean the words and want to do what is done (No. 3).

Oscar O'Toole told me: "I'm so mad at my son, Father, that I won't even sit with him in church—that way I don't feel so bad about hating him when we're singing all those songs about love and . . ."

Hating him?

Jesus asks us still:

"Would any of you who are fathers give your son a stone when he asks you for bread? Or would you give him a snake when he asks you for a fish?" (Mt 7:9-10).

God asks us still:

Does a woman forget her baby at the breast,
or fail to cherish the son of her womb?
Yet even if these forget,
I will never forget you (Is 49:15, *JB*).

Music in Catholic Worship says:

We come together to acknowledge the love of God poured out among us in the work of the Spirit, to stand in awe and praise (No. 2).

But how can we possibly do that when we're mad at one another? We are only human after all, aren't we—Marjorie and Harvey and Oscar and you and I? Forgiveness and reconciliation are godlike qualities. Aren't they really too difficult for us? Wouldn't it be easier for us not to get personally involved—to be physically present at eucharistic celebrations but emotionally detached?

Music in Catholic Worship says:

In true celebration each sign or sacramental action will be invested with the personal and prayerful faith, care, attention, and enthusiasm of those who carry it out (No. 9).

There is a wonderful story I remember from Francois Mauriac's *Woman of the Pharisees* which helps me understand the problem of love and hate, the problem of reconciliation and forgiveness, the problem of that knot of tears in our throat that prevents us from saying or singing, "I'm sorry."

As I recall the story, Mauriac tells of a little boy whose mother has no time for him. She's always getting all dressed up and going out, leaving him alone. He reaches after her, time and time again, but she's always gone.

One day the boy gets on his bicycle and follows his mother's horse and carriage as she's leaving. She goes to a nearby town. He follows. She goes into an apartment building. He waits across the alley. And he waits and waits. He waits all night, finally falling asleep, leaning against his bike in a doorway across the alley from the house his mother entered.

The boy is awakened by the sounds of laughter. He looks up. It is early morning. And there, in a balcony window across the way is his mother. She is with a strange man. And they have obviously spent the night together.

The boy pedals home furiously. He is hurt and angry. He meets the parish priest, who has befriended him before, and he finally allows himself to cry. "I hate her," he yells. "I hate her, Father. I guess you don't believe me. You think I don't really mean it. But I do. I really hate her."

"I know," the priest says to the little boy. "Our Lord tells us to love our enemies. It is often easier to do that—than not to hate those we love."

"Yes," the boy sobs, "because they can hurt you so much. . . ."

Mauriac's insight is powerful. Aren't the people we love really the only people who can hurt us, the only people to whom we are deeply vulnerable? And so, it is often easier to love our enemies than it is not to hate people we love. It is often easier for me to act lovingly toward a stranger than it is for me to keep myself from hating a relative.

I'm sorry I can't sing "I'm sorry"

I'm sitting on a bus in Manhattan. An enormous hulk of a man, obviously on his way to try out for the part of King Kong in some off-off Broadway musical extravaganza, stands in front of me. Then he stands on me. His foot is on my foot. My right foot is a huge, throbbing, purple pancake.

"Oops, sorry," he says.

Two words: one word is "oops" and the other is "sorry."

What do I say to that? Oh, something wonderful like, "Oh, don't mention it. . . . I have another foot just like it. . . . Perfectly all right. . . . Besides, it's my right foot anyway and I'm left-footed. . . . Yes, I'm a left-footed person. . . . Perfectly all right. . . ."

But suppose one Sunday at a family birthday get-together my favorite sister says to me, "Hey, brother, you're putting on a little weight there, aren't you? Maybe a little too much pasta in the pot?"

What do I say to that? Oh, something wonderful like, "And so who are you? My sister the scale?. . . . I need you to tell me how much I weigh?. . . . You're not exactly Mia Farrow either, Sweetheart. . . ." Humph! I hope she doesn't think she's getting a Christmas card from me this year!

How hard it is to be reconciled with those we love.

> So if you are about to offer your gift to God at the altar and there you remember that your brother has something against you, leave your gift there in front of the altar, go at once and make peace with your brother, and then come back and offer your gift to God (Mt 5:23-24).

Maybe I'll give her a bathroom scale for Christmas. Too much pasta! What does she mean too much pasta? In the whole world, there couldn't possibly be too much pasta.

And how frequently the grief goes round in circles. The boss yells at Daddy, Daddy comes home mad and shouts to Mommy, "How many times do I have to tell you that I don't like chicken cutlets on Thursdays in April?"

Mommy says to Baby, "And if you don't eat every last bit of that mashed cauliflower and kidney beans, you'll be sorry, Baby."

Baby chokes down the cauliflower and kidney bean combo and goes into the living room where he kicks the dog who growls at the cat who snarls at the goldfish who spits at Daddy who yells at Mommy who starts mashing more cauliflower and kidney beans for Baby who . . .

Your Abba has forgiven you such an enormous debt. Can't you forgive one another those petty, little, nickle-and-dime I.O.U.s?

But I'm right and he's wrong. So what? Being right isn't what matters in loving relationships. Loving is what matters. Forgiveness matters. Reconciliation matters. And our liturgies today don't let us forget it.

> "Receive the Holy Spirit. If you forgive people's sins, they are forgiven; if you do not forgive them, they are not forgiven."

That's what Jesus tells us, his disciples, in John 20:22-23.

"You mean, if I forgive my mother-in-law, God forgives her. If I don't, then God . . ."

It certainly sounds like that, doesn't it? Do we believe it?

> "Our Father . . .
> Forgive us the wrongs we have done,
> as we forgive the wrongs that others have done to us" (Mt 6:12).

Do we believe that? Don't we really want and expect God to be much more forgiving than we are? Please, God, don't take that prayer literally.

> "If you forgive others the wrongs they have done to you, your Father in heaven will also forgive you. But if you do not forgive others, then your Father will not forgive the wrongs you have done" (Mt 6:14-15).

Maybe Jesus did mean it all literally. Didn't he himself pray from the cross:

> "Forgive them, Father! They don't know what they are doing" (Lk 23:34)?

And, after his resurrection, when he came back to see his friends, what did Jesus do? He would have been perfectly within his rights to have said to them: "And where were you? You're supposed to be my friends. How could you have deserted me? How . . ." He could have said something like that. After all, he was "right" and they were "wrong."

But all Jesus says is "Shalom . . . Peace. . . ." John reminds us:

> Jesus said to them again, "Peace be with you. As the Father sent me, so I send you." Then he breathed on them and said, "Receive the Holy Spirit. If you forgive people's sins, they are forgiven; if you do not forgive them, they are not forgiven" (Jn 20:21-23).

"Peace . . . Shalom . . . Forgive. . . ."

How can we forgive as the Father forgives us? How can we forgive as Jesus forgives us? It helps to pray for the people we are trying to forgive. It helps especially to pray at eucharistic celebrations. That is where sins are forgiven and we are reconciled with one another and with God.

Besides, when we pray for our relatives and friends, we do more than ask God's help for them. We also remind ourselves that our relatives and friends need God's help, that they are human, that they aren't perfect. That reminder is an important first step in reconciliation.

Music in Catholic Worship says, "Christians gather at Mass that they may hear and express their faith again in this assembly and, by expressing it, renew and deepen it" (No. 1).

We all need to express and renew and deepen our faith. We are all imperfect human beings: Marjorie and Mortimer, Harvey and Gus, Oscar and his son, you and I.

So your mother drives you crazy. So what? So she keeps forgetting your name. She's not perfect. So she calls you Jennifer and your name is Harry. She's only human.

Pray for her. Pray for her that you will be better able to accept her humanness and her struggling Christianness and forgive her and accept her and be reconciled.

Sing your prayers at Mass for her. Sing your prayers at Mass *with* her. Really celebrate the Eucharist with her . . . and me and Mabel McGillicuddy and Bobby Baccigalupo, and Marjorie and Mortimer, Harvey and Gus, Oscar and his son—and Jesus and his Abba and their Spirit.

Then there will be love.

And that's what we've been singing about in our eucharistic celebrations all along.

Music in Catholic Worship

Bishops' Committee On the Liturgy

Introduction

In November 1967, the Bishops' Committee on the Liturgy published a statement on music entitled "The Place of Music in Eucharistic Celebrations." This statement was drawn up after study by the then Music Advisory Board and submitted to the Bishops' Committee on the Liturgy. The Bishops' Committee approved the statement, adopted it as its own, and recommended it for consideration by all. The following statement on music in liturgical celebrations is a further development of that statement and was drawn up after study by the committee on music of the National Federation of Diocesan Liturgical Commissions. Their work was reviewed by the Bishops' Committee on the Liturgy and their advisors. The finished copy is presented to all by the Bishops' Committee on the Liturgy as background and guidelines for the proper role of music within the liturgy.

In the course of this century music and its role in the liturgy have been the subject of many documents. On November 22, 1903, the motu proprio *Tra le Sollecitudini* of Saint Pius X was promulgated; on December 20, 1928, the apostolic constitution of Pope Pius XI, *Divini cultus,* was published; the encyclical of Pope Pius XII, *Musicae sacrae disciplina,* was promulgated on December 25, 1955. On September 3, 1958, the Congregation of Rites issued an instruction on sacred music and the sacred liturgy. The crescendo of documents, both major and minor, on the role of music in the liturgy continued and reached the culminating point in Vatican II's Constitution on the Liturgy in which an entire chapter was dedicated to sacred music. The liturgical constitution explained the role of music in divine services and formulated a number of principles and guidelines on this subject. Next, on March 5, 1967, the Consilium—the post-conciliar commission on the reform of the liturgy—in conjunction with the Congregation of Rites issued an instruction on music in the liturgy. The latter prompted the former statement of the Bishops' Committee on the Liturgy, "The Place of Music in Eucharistic Celebrations."

A few years have elapsed, and the pastoral situation in the United States can be regarded with greater calm and serenity. However, it is urgent that fresh guidelines be given to foster interest with regard to music in the liturgy.

After several years with the 1967 statement it should now be clear that mere observance of a pattern or rule of sung liturgy will not create a living and authentic celebration of worship in Christian congregations. That is the reason why statements such as this must take the form of recommendations and attempts at guidance. In turn, this demands responsible study and choice by priests and leaders of singing: "a very wide field of diverse liturgical practice is now open, within the limits set by the present discipline and regulations . . . Not all priests appreciate how wide the opportunities are for planning lively and intelligible celebrations" (National Conference of Catholic Bishops, April 1967)—especially in the various combinations of song and spoken prayer in the liturgy.

It is hoped that this statement of the Bishops' Committee on the Liturgy will be of use to the bishops and their liturgical commissions and to all who celebrate or plan liturgies.

Music in Catholic Worship

I. THE THEOLOGY OF CELEBRATION

1. A man is a Christian because through the Christian community he has met Jesus Christ, heard his word in invitation, and responded to him in faith. Christians gather at Mass that they may hear and express their faith again in this assembly and, by expressing it, renew and deepen it.

2. We do not come to meet Christ as if he were absent from the rest of our lives. We come together to deepen our awareness of, and commitment to, the action of his Spirit in the whole of our lives at every moment. We come together to acknowledge the love of God poured out among us in the work of the Spirit, to stand in awe and praise.

3. We are celebrating when we involve ourselves meaningfully in the thoughts, words, songs, and gestures of the worshipping community—when everything we do is wholehearted and authentic for us—when we mean the words and want to do what is done.

4. People in love make signs of love, not only to express their love but also to deepen it. Love never expressed dies. Christians' love for Christ and for each other, Christians' faith in Christ and in each other, must be expressed in the signs and symbols of celebration or it will die.

5. Celebrations need not fail, even on a particular Sunday when our feelings do not match the invitation of Christ and his Church to worship. Faith does not always permeate our feelings. But the sign and symbols of worship can give bodily expression to faith as we celebrate. Our own faith is stimulated. We become one with others whose faith is similarly expressed. We rise above our own feelings to respond to God in prayer.

6. Faith grows when it is well expressed in celebration. Good celebrations foster and nourish faith. Poor celebrations weaken and destroy faith.

7. To celebrate the liturgy means to do the action or perform the sign in such a way that the full meaning and impact shine forth in clear and compelling fashion. Since these signs are vehicles of communication and instruments of faith, they must be simple and comprehensible. Since they are directed to fellow human beings, they must be humanly attractive. They must be meaningful and appealing to the body of worshippers or they will fail to stir up faith and men will fail to worship the Father.

8. The signs of celebration should be short, clear and unencumbered by useless repetition; they should be "within the people's power of comprehension and normally should not require much explanation."[1]

If the signs need explanation to communicate faith, they will often be watched instead of celebrated.

9. In true celebration each sign or sacramental action will be invested with the personal and prayerful faith, care, attention, and enthusiasm of those who carry it out.

II. PASTORAL PLANNING FOR CELEBRATION

10. The responsibility for effective pastoral celebration in a parish community falls upon all those who exercise major roles in the liturgy. "The particular preparation for each liturgical celebration should be done in a spirit of cooperation by all parties concerned, under the guidance of the rector of the church, whether it be ritual, pastoral, or musical matters."[2] In practice this ordinarily means an organized "planning team" or committee which meets regularly to achieve creative and coordinated worship and a good use of the liturgical and musical options of a flexible liturgy.

11. The power of a liturgical celebration to share faith will frequently depend upon its unity—a unity drawn from the liturgical feast or season or from the readings appointed in the lectionary and artistic unity flowing from the skillful and sensitive selection of options, music, and related arts. The sacred scriptures ought to be the source and inspiration of sound planning for it is the very nature of celebration that men hear the saving words and works of the Lord and then respond in meaningful signs and symbols. Where the readings of the lectionary possess a thematic unity the other elements ought to be so arranged as to constitute a setting for and response to the message of the Word.

12. The planning team or committee is headed by the priest (celebrant and homilist) for no congregation can experience the security of a unified celebration if that unity is not grasped by the one who presides, as well as by those who have special roles. It should include those with the knowledge and artistic skills needed in celebration—men and women trained in music, poetry, and art, and knowledge in current resources in these areas—men and women sensitive to the present-day thirst of so many for the riches of scripture, theology, and prayer. It is always good to include some members of the congregation who have not taken special roles in the celebrations so that honest evaluations can be made.

13. The planning should go beyond the choosing of options, songs, and ministers to the composition of such texts as the brief introduction, general intercessions, and other appropriate comments as provided in the General Instruction of the Roman Missal. The manner of inviting the people to join in a particular song may be as important as the choice of the song itself.

14. In planning pastoral celebrations the congregation, the occasion, and the celebrant must be taken into consideration.

The Congregation

15. "The pastoral effectiveness of a celebration depends in great measure on choosing readings, prayers, and songs which correspond to the needs, spiritual preparation, and attitudes of the participants."[3] A type of celebration suitable for a youth group may not fit in a retirement home; a more formal style effective in a parish church may be inappropriate in a home liturgy. The music used should be within the competence of most of the worshippers. It should suit their age level, cultural background, and level of faith.

16. Variation in level of faith raises special problems. Liturgical celebration presupposes a minimum of biblical knowledge and a deep commitment of living faith. Lacking these conditions, the liturgy may be forced to become a tool of evangelization. Greater liberty in the choice of music and style of celebration may be required as the participants are led toward that day when they can share a growing faith in the whole community. Songs like the psalms may create rather than solve problems where faith is weak. Music, chosen with care, can serve as a bridge to faith as well as an expression of it.

17. The diversity of people present at a parish liturgy gives rise to a further problem. Can the same parish liturgy be an authentic expression for a grade school girl, her college-age brother, their married sister with her young family, their parents and grandparents? Can it satisfy the theologically and musically educated along with those lacking in training? Can it please those who seek a more informal style of celebration? The planning team must consider the general makeup of the total community. Each Christian must keep in mind that to live and worship in community often demands a personal sacrifice. Everyone must be willing to share likes and dislikes with those whose ideas and experience may be quite unlike his own.

18. Often the problem of diversity can be mitigated by supplementing the parish Sunday celebration with special celebrations for smaller homogeneous groups. "The need of the faithful of a particular cultural background or of a particular age level may often be met by a music that can serve as a congenial, liturgical oriented expression of prayer."[4] The music and other options may then be more easily suited to the particular group celebrating. Nevertheless, it would be out of harmony with the Lord's wish for unity in his Church if believers were to worship only in such homogeneous groupings.[5] Celebration in such groups, "in which the genuine sense of community is more readily experienced, can contribute significantly to growth in awareness of the parish as community, especially when all the faithful participate in the parish Mass on the Lord's day."[6]

The Occasion

19. The same congregation will want to celebrate in a variety of ways. During the course of the year the different mysteries of redemption are celebrated at Mass so that in some way they are made present.[7] Each feast and season has its own spirit and its own music. The penitential occasions demand more restraint. The great feasts demand more solemnity. Solemnity, however, depends less on the ornateness of song and magnificence of ceremonial than on worthy and religious celebration.[8]

20. Generally a congregation or choir will want to sing more on the great feasts like Christmas and Easter and less in the season through the year. Important events in family and parish life will suggest fuller programs of song. Sundays will be celebrated with variety but always as befits the day of the Lord. All liturgies, from the very simple to the most ornate, must be truly pastoral and prayerful.

The Celebrant

21. No other single factor affects the liturgy as much as the attitude, style, and bearing of the celebrant: his sincere faith and warmth as he welcomes the worshipping community; his human naturalness combined with dignity and seriousness as he breaks the Bread of Word and Eucharist.

22. The style and pattern of song ought to facilitate the effectiveness of a good celebrant. His role is enhanced when he is capable of rendering some of his parts in song and he should be encouraged to do so. What he cannot sing well and effectively he ought to recite. If capable of singing, he ought, for the sake of people, to rehearse carefully the sung parts that would contribute to their celebration.[9]

III. THE PLACE OF MUSIC IN THE CELEBRATION

Music Serves the Expression of Faith

23. Among the many signs and symbols used by the Church to celebrate its faith, music is of preeminent importance. As sacred song united to the words it forms an integral part of solemn liturgy.[10] Yet the function of music is ministerial; it must serve and never dominate. Music should assist the assembled believers to express and share the gift of faith that is within them and to nourish and strengthen their interior commitment of faith. It should heighten the texts so that they speak more fully and more effectively. The quality of joy and enthusiasm which music adds to community worship cannot be gained in any other way. It imparts a sense of unity to the congregation and sets the appropriate tone for a particular celebration.

24. Music, in addition to expressing texts, can also unveil a dimension of meaning and feeling, a communication of ideas and intuitions which words alone cannot yield. This dimension is integral to the human personality and to man's growth in faith. It cannot be ignored if the signs of worship are to speak to the whole person. Ideally every communal celebration of faith, including funerals and the sacraments of baptism, confirmation, penance, anointing and matrimony, should include music and singing. Where the Liturgy of the Hours is able to be celebrated in a community, it too should include music.

Evaluation of Music in Celebration

25. To determine the value of a given musical element in a liturgical celebration a threefold judgment must be made: musical, liturgical, and pastoral.

The Musical Judgment

26. Is the music technically, aesthetically, and expressively good? This judgment is basic and primary and should be made by competent musicians. Only artistically sound music will be effective in the long run. To admit the cheap, the trite, the musical cliche often found in popular songs on the grounds of instant liturgy is to cheapen the liturgy, to expose it to ridicule, and to invite failure.

27. Musicians must search for and create music of quality for worship, especially the new musical settings for the new liturgical texts. They must also do the research needed to find new uses for the best of the old music. They must explore the repertory of good music used in other communions. They must find practical means of preserving and using our rich heritage of Latin chants and motets.[11]

In the meantime, however, the words of St. Augustine should not be forgotten: "Do not allow yourselves to be offended by the imperfect while you strive for the perfect."

28. We do a disservice to musical values, however, when we confuse the judgment of music with the judgment of musical style. Style and value are two distinct judgments. Good music of new styles is finding a happy home in the celebrations of today. To chant and polyphony we have effectively added the chorale hymn, restored responsorial singing to some extent, and employed many styles of contemporary composition. Music in folk idiom is finding acceptance in eucharistic celebrations. We must judge value within each style.

"In modern times the Church has consistently recognized and freely admitted the use of various styles of music as an aid to liturgical worship. Since the promulgation of the Constitution on the Liturgy and more especially since the introduction of vernacular languages into the liturgy, there has arisen a more pressing need for musical compositions in idioms that can be sung by the congregation and thus further communal participation."[12]

29. The musician has every right to insist that the music be good. But although all liturgical music should be good music, not all good music is suitable to the liturgy. The musical judgment is basic but not final. There remain the liturgical and pastoral judgments.

THE LITURGICAL JUDGMENT

30. The nature of the liturgy itself will help to determine what kind of music is called for, what parts are to be preferred for singing and who is to sing them.

Structural Requirements

31. The choice of sung parts, the balance between them and the style of musical setting used should reflect the relative importance of the parts of the Mass (or other service) and the nature of each part. Thus elaborate settings of the entrance song, "Lord Have Mercy" and "Glory to God" may make the proclamation of the word seem unimportant; an overly elaborate offertory song with a spoken "Holy, Holy, Holy Lord" may make the eucharistic prayer seem less important.

Textual Requirements

32. Does the music express and interpret the text correctly and make it more meaningful? Is the form of the text respected? In making these judgments the principal classes of texts must be kept in mind: proclamations, acclamations, psalms and hymns, and prayers. Each has a specific function which must be served by the music chosen for a text.

In most instances there is an official liturgical text approved by the episcopal conference. "Vernacular texts set to music composed in earlier periods," however, "may be used in liturgical texts."[13] As noted elsewhere, criteria have been provided for the texts which may replace the processional chants of Mass. In these cases and in the choice of all supplementary music, the texts "must always be in conformity with Catholic doctrine; indeed they should be drawn chiefly from holy scripture and from liturgical sources."[14]

Role Differentiation

33. "In liturgical celebrations each person, minister or layman, who has an office to perform, should do all of, but only, those parts which pertain to his office by the nature of the rite and the principles of liturgy."[15] Special musical concern must be given to the roles of the congregation, the cantor, the choir and the instrumentalists.

The Congregation

34. Music for the congregation must be within the performance ability of the members of the congregation. The congregation must be comfortable and secure with what they are doing in order to celebrate well.

The Cantor

35. While there is no place in the liturgy for display of virtuosity for its own sake, artistry is valued, and an individual singer can effectively lead the assembly, attractively proclaim the Word of God in the psalm sung between the readings and take his part in other responsorial singing. "Provision should be made for at least one or two properly trained singers, especially where there is no possibility of setting up even a small choir." The singer will present some simpler musical setting, with the people taking part, and can lead and support the faithful as far as is needed. The presence of such a singer is desirable even in churches which have a choir for those celebrations in which the choir cannot take part, but which may fittingly be performed with some solemnity and therefore with singing."[16] Although a cantor "cannot enhance the service of worship in the same way as a choir, a trained and competent cantor can perform an important ministry by leading the congregation in common sacred song and in responsorial singing."[17]

The Choir

36. A well-trained choir adds beauty and solemnity to the liturgy and also assists and encourages the singing of the congregation. The Second Vatican Council, in speaking of the choir, stated emphatically: "Choirs must be diligently promoted" provided that "the whole body of the faithful may be able to contribute that active participation which is rightly theirs."[18]

"At times the choir, within the congregation of the faithful and as part of it, will assume the role of leadership, while at other times it will retain its own distinctive ministry. This means that the choir will lead the people in sung prayer, by alternating or reinforcing the sacred song of the congregation, or by enhancing it with the addition of a musical elaboration. At other times in the course of liturgical celebration, the choir alone will sing works whose musical demands enlist and challenge its competence."[19]

The Organist and Other Instrumentalists

37. Singing is not the only kind of music suitable for liturgical celebration. Music performed on the organ and other instruments can stimulate feelings of joy and contemplation at appropriate times.[20] This can be done effectively at the following points: an instrumental prelude, a soft background to a spoken psalm, at the preparation of the gifts in place of singing, during portions of the communion rite, and the recessional.

In the dioceses of the United States, "musical instruments other than the organ may be used in liturgical services, provided they are played in a manner that is suitable to public worship."[21] This decision deliberately refrains from singling out specific instruments. Their use depends on circumstances, the nature of the congregation, etc.

38. The *proper placing* of the organ and choir according to the arrangement and acoustics of the church will facilitate celebration. Practically speaking, the choir must be near the director and the organ (both console and sound). The choir ought to be able to perform without too much distraction; the acoustics ought to give a lively presence of sound in the choir area and allow both tone and word to reach the congregation with clarity. Visually it is desirable that the choir appear to be part of the worshipping community, yet a part which serves in a unique way. Locating the organ console too far from the congregation causes a time lag which tends to make the singing drag unless the organist is trained to cope with it. A location near the front pews will facilitate congregational singing.

THE PASTORAL JUDGMENT

39. The pastoral judgment governs the use and function of every element of celebration. Ideally this judgment is made by the planning team or committee. It is the judgment that must be made in this particular situation, in these concrete circumstances. Does music in the celebration enable these people to express their faith, in this place, in this age, in this culture?

40. The instruction of the Congregation for Divine Worship, issued September 5, 1971, encourages episcopal conferences to consider not only liturgical music's suitability to the time and circumstances of the celebration, "but also the needs of the faithful who will sing them. All means must be used to promote singing by the people. New forms should be used, which are adapted to the different mentalities and to modern tastes." The document adds that the music and the instruments "should correspond to the sacred character of the celebration and the place of worship."

41. A musician may judge that a certain composition or style of composition is good music but his musical judgment really says nothing about whether and how this music is to be used in this celebration. The signs of the celebration must be accepted and received as meaningful for a genuinely human faith experience for these specific worshippers. This pastoral judgment can be aided by sociological studies of the people who make up the congregation: their age culture, and education. These factors influence the effectiveness of the liturgical signs, including music. No set of rubrics or regulations of itself will ever achieve a truly pastoral celebration of the sacramental rites. Such regulations must always be applied with a pastoral concern for the given worshipping community.

IV. GENERAL CONSIDERATION ON LITURGICAL STRUCTURE

42. Those who are responsible for planning the music for eucharistic celebrations in accord with the three judgments above must have a clear understanding of the structure of the liturgy. They must be aware of what is the primary importance. They should know the nature of each of the parts of the liturgy and the relationship of each part to the overall rhythm of the liturgical action.

43. The Mass is made up of the liturgy of the word and the liturgy of the Eucharist. These two parts are so closely connected as to form one act of worship. The table of the Lord is the table of God's Word and Christ's Body, and from it the faithful are instructed and refreshed. In addition, the Mass has introductory and concluding rites.[22] The introductory and concluding rites are secondary.

The Introductory Rites

44. The parts preceding the liturgy of the word, namely, the entrance, greeting, penitential rite, Kyrie, Gloria, and opening prayer or collect, have the character of introduction and preparation. The purpose of these rites is to help the assembled people become a worshipping community and to prepare them for listening to God's Word and celebrating the Eucharist.[23] Of these parts the entrance song and the opening prayer are primary. All else is secondary.

If Mass begins with the sprinkling of the people with blessed water, the penitential rite is omitted; this may be done at all Sunday Masses.[24] Similarly, if the psalms of part of the Liturgy of the Hours precede Mass, the introductory rite is abbreviated in accord with the General Instruction on the office of prayer.[25]

The Liturgy of the Word

45. Readings from scripture are the heart of the liturgy of the word. The homily, responsorial psalms, profession of faith, and general intercessions develop and complete it. In the readings, God speaks to his people and nourishes their spirit; Christ is present through his word. The homily explains the readings. The chants and the profession of faith comprise the people's acceptance of God's Word. It is of primary importance that the people hear God's message of love, digest it with the aid of psalms, silence, and the homily, and respond, involving themselves in the great covenant of love and redemption. All else is secondary.

The Preparation of the Gifts

46. The eucharistic prayer is preceded by the preparation of the gifts. The purpose of the rite is to prepare bread and wine for the sacrifice. The secondary character of the rite determines the manner of the celebration. It consists very simply of bringing the gifts to the altar, possibly accompanied by song, prayers to be said by the celebrant as he prepares the gifts, and the prayer over the gifts. Of these elements the bringing of the gifts, the placing of the gifts on the altar, and the prayer over the gifts are primary. All else is secondary.

The Eucharistic Prayer

47. The eucharistic prayer, a prayer of thanksgiving and sanctification, is the center of the entire celebration. By an introductory dialogue the priest invites the people to lift their hearts to God in praise and thanks; he unites them with himself in the prayer he addresses in their name to the Father through Jesus Christ. The meaning of the prayer is that the whole congregation joins Christ in acknowledging the works of God and offering the sacrifice.[26] As a statement of the faith of the local assembly it is affirmed and ratified by all those present through acclamations of faith: the first acclamation or Sanctus, the memorial acclamation, and the Great Amen.

The Communion Rite

48. The eating and drinking of the Body and Blood of the Lord in a paschal meal is the climax of our eucharistic celebration. It is prepared for by several rites: the Lord's Prayer with embolism and doxology, the rite of peace, breaking of bread (and commingling) during the "Lamb of God," private preparation of the priest and showing of the eucharistic bread. The eating and drinking is accompanied by a song expressing the unity of communicants and is followed by a time of prayer after communion.[27] Those elements are primary which show forth signs that the first fruit of the Eucharist is the unity of the Body of Christ, Christians loving Christ through loving one another. The principal texts to accompany or express the sacred action are the Lord's Prayer, the song during the communion procession, and the prayer after communion.

The Concluding Rite

49. The concluding rite consists of the priest's greeting and blessing, which is sometimes expanded by the prayer over the people or another solemn form, and the dismissal which sends each member of the congregation to do good works, praising and blessing the Lord.[28]

A recessional song is optional. The greeting, blessing, dismissal, and recessional song or instrumental music ideally form one continuous action which may culminate in the priest's personal greetings and conversations at the church door.

V. APPLICATION OF THE PRINCIPLES OF CELEBRATION TO MUSIC IN EUCHARISTIC WORSHIP

General Considerations

50. Many and varied musical patterns are now possible within the liturgical structure. Musicians and composers need to respond creatively and responsibly to the challenge of developing new music for today's celebrations.

51. While it is possible to make technical distinctions in the forms of Mass—all the way from the Mass in which nothing is sung to the Mass in which everything is sung—such distinctions are of little significance in themselves; almost unlimited combinations of sung and recited parts may be chosen. The important decision is whether or not this or that part may or should be sung in this particular celebration and under these specific circumstances.[29] The former distinction between the ordinary and proper parts of the Mass with regard to musical settings and distribution of roles is no longer retained. For this reason the musical settings of the past are usually not helpful models for composing truly liturgical contemporary pieces.

52. Two patterns used to serve as foundation for the creating and planning of liturgy: One was "High Mass" with its five movements, sung Ordinary and fourfold sung Proper. The other was the four-hymn "Low Mass" format that grew out of the Instruction on Sacred Music of 1958. The four-hymn pattern developed in the context of a Latin Mass which could accommodate song in the vernacular only at certain points. It is now outdated and the Mass has more than a dozen parts that may be sung as well as numerous options for the celebrant. Each of these parts must be understood according to its proper nature and function.

Specific Applications

The Acclamations

53. The acclamations are shouts of joy which arise from the whole assembly as forceful and meaningful assents to God's Word and Action. They are important because they make some of the most significant moments of the Mass (gospel, eucharistic prayer, Lord's Prayer) stand out. It is of their nature that they be rhythmically strong, melodically appealing, and affirmative. The people should know the acclamations by heart in order to sing them spontaneously. Some variety is recommended and even imperative. The challenge to the composer and people alike is one of variety without confusion.

54. In the eucharistic celebration there are five acclamations which ought to be sung even at Masses in which little else is sung: Alleluia, "Holy, Holy, Holy Lord;" Memorial Acclamation; Great Amen; Doxology to the Lord's Prayer.

The Alleluia

55. This acclamation of paschal joy is both a reflection upon the Word of God proclaimed in the Liturgy and a preparation for the gospel. All stand to sing it. After the cantor or choir sings the alleluia(s), the people customarily repeat it. Then a single proper verse is sung by the cantor or choir, and all repeat the alleluia(s). If not sung, the alleluia may be omitted.[30] In its place a moment of silent reflection may be observed. During Lent a brief verse of acclamatory character replaces the alleluia and is sung in the same way.

"Holy, Holy, Holy Lord"

56. This is the people's acclamation of praise concluding the preface of the eucharistic prayer. We join the whole communion of saints in acclaiming the Lord. Settings which add harmony or descants on solemn feasts and occasions are appropriate, but since this chant belongs to priest and people, the choir parts must facilitate and make effective the people's parts.

The Memorial Acclamations

57. We support one another's faith in the paschal mystery, the central mystery of our belief. This acclamation is properly a memorial of the Lord's suffering and glorification with an expression of faith in his coming, but variety in text and music is desirable.

The Great Amen

58. The worshippers assent to the eucharistic prayer and make it their own in the Great Amen. To be most effective, the Amen may be repeated or augmented. Choirs may harmonize and expand upon the people's acclamation.

Doxology to the Lord's Prayer

59. These words of praise, "For the Kingdom, the power and the glory is yours, now and forever," are fittingly sung by all especially when the Lord's Prayer is sung. Here too the choir may enhance the acclamation with harmony.

THE PROCESSIONAL SONGS

60. The two processional chants—the entrance song and the communion song—are very important for a sense of awareness of community. Proper antiphons are given to be used with appropriate psalm verses. These may be replaced by the chants of the *Simple Gradual,* by other psalms and antiphons, or by other fitting songs.[31]

The entrance song

61. The entrance song should create an atmosphere of celebration. It serves the function of putting the assembly in the proper frame of mind for listening to the Word of God. It helps people to become conscious of themselves as a worshipping community. The choice of texts for the entrance song should not conflict with these purposes. In general, during the most important seasons of the Church year, Easter, Lent, Christmas and Advent, it is preferable that most songs used at the entrance be seasonal in nature.[32]

The communion song

62. The communion should foster a sense of unity. It should be simple and not demand great effort. It gives expression to the joy of unity in the body of Christ and the fulfillment of the mystery being celebrated. Most benediction hymns, by reason of their concentration on adoration rather than on communion, are not acceptable. In general, during the most important seasons of the Church year, Easter, Lent, Christmas, and Advent, it is preferable that most songs used at the communion be seasonal in nature. During the remainder of the Church year, however, topical songs may be used during the communion procession, provided these texts do not conflict with the paschal character of every Sunday."[33]

RESPONSORIAL PSALMS

63. This unique and very important song is the response to the first lesson. The new lectionary lists 900 refrains in its determination to match the content of the psalms to the theme of reading. The liturgy of the Word comes to life if between the first two readings a cantor sings the psalm and all sing the response. Since most groups cannot learn a new response every week, seasonal refrains are offered in the lectionary itself and in the *Simple Gradual.* Other psalms and refrains may also be used, including psalms arranged in responsorial form, metrical and similar versions of psalms, provided they are used in accordance with the principles of the *Simple Gradual* and are selected in harmony with the liturgical season, feast or occasion. The choice of the texts which are not from the psalter is not extended to the chants between the readings.[34] To facilitate reflection, there may be a brief period of silence between the first reading and the responsorial psalm.

ORDINARY CHANTS

64. The fourth category is the ordinary chants which now may be treated as individual choices. One or more may be sung, the others spoken. The pattern may vary according to the circumstances. These chants are as follows:

Lord have mercy

65. This short litany was traditionally a prayer of praise to the risen Christ. He has been raised and made "Lord" and we beg him to show his loving kindness. The sixfold Kyrie of the new Order of Mass may be sung in other ways, for example, as a ninefold chant.[35] It may also be incorporated in the penitential rite, with invocations addressed to Christ. When sung, the setting should be brief and simple so as not to give undue importance to the introductory rites.

"Glory to God"

66. This ancient hymn of praise is now given in a new

poetic and singable translation. It may be introduced by celebrant, cantor or choir. The restricted use of the Gloria, i.e., only on Sundays outside Advent and Lent and on solemnities and feasts,[36] emphasizes its special and solemn character. The new text offers many opportunities for alternation of choir and people in poetic parallelisms. The "Glory to God" also provides an opportunity for the choir to sing alone on festive occasions.

Lord's Prayer

67. This prayer begins our immediate preparation for sharing in the Paschal Banquet. The traditional text is retained and may be set to music by composers with the same freedom as other parts of the Ordinary. All settings must provide for the participation of the priest and all present.

"Lamb of God"

68. The Agnus Dei is a litany-song to accompany the breaking of the bread, in preparation for communion. The invocation and response may be repeated as the action demands. The final response is always "grant us peace." Unlike the "Holy, Holy, Holy Lord," and the Lord's Prayer, the "Lamb of God" is not necessarily a song of the people. Hence it may be sung by the choir, though the people should generally make the response.

Profession of Faith

69. This is a communal profession of faith in which ". . . the people who have heard the Word of God in the lesson and in the homily may assent and respond to it, and may renew in themselves the rule of faith as they begin to celebrate the Eucharist."[37] It is usually preferable that the Creed be spoken in declamatory fashion rather than sung.[38] If it is sung, it might more effectively take the form of a simple musical declamation rather than that of an extensive and involved musical structure.

Supplementary Songs

70. This category includes songs for which there are no specified texts nor any requirement that there should be a spoken or sung text. Here the choir may play a fuller role for there is no question of usurping the people's parts. This category includes the following:

The Offertory Song

71. The offertory song may accompany the procession and preparation of the gifts. It is not always necessary or desirable. Organ or instrumental music is also fitting at the time. When song is used it is to be noted that the song need not speak of bread and wine or of offering. The proper function of this song is to accompany and celebrate the communal aspects of the procession. The text, therefore, can be any appropriate song of praise or of rejoicing in keeping with the season. The antiphons of the Roman Gradual, not included in the new Roman Missal, may be used with psalm vocals. Instrumental interludes can effectively accompany the procession of preparation of the gifts and thus keep this part of the Mass in proper perspective relative to the eucharistic prayer which follows.

The Psalm or Song after Communion

72. The singing of a psalm or hymn of praise after the distribution of communion is optional. If the organ is played or the choir sings during the distribution of communion, a congregational song may well provide a fitting expression of oneness in the Eucharistic Lord. Since no particular text is specified, there is ample room for creativity.

The Recessional Song

73. The recessional song has never been an official part of the rite; hence musicians are free to plan music which provides an appropriate closing to the liturgy. A song is one possible choice. However, if the people have sung a song after communion, it may be advisable to use only an instrumental or choir recessional.

Litanies

74. Litanies are often more effective when sung. The repetition of melody and rhythm draws the people together in a strong and unified response. In addition to the "Lamb of God," already mentioned, the general intercessions (prayer of the faithful) offer an opportunity for litanical singing, as do the invocations of Christ in the penitential rite.

Progress and New Directions

75. Many new patterns and combinations of song are emerging in eucharistic celebrations. Congregations most frequently sing an entrance song, alleluia, "Holy, Holy, Holy Lord," memorial acclamation, Great Amen, and a song at communion (or a song after communion). Other parts are added in varying quantities, depending on season, degree of solemnity and musical resources. Choirs often add one or more of the following: a song before Mass, an Offertory song, the "Glory to God" on special occasions, additional communion songs or a song after communion or a recessional. They may also enhance the congregationally sung entrance song and acclamations with descants, harmony, and antiphonal arrangements. Harmony is desirable when it gives breadth and power to the unison voice of people without confusing them.

76. Flexibility reigns supreme. The musician with a sense of artistry and a deep knowledge of the rhythm of the liturgical action will be able to combine the many options into an effective whole. For the composer and performer alike there is an unprecedented challenge. He must enhance the liturgy with new creations of variety and richness and with those compositions from the time-honored treasury of liturgical music which can still serve today's celebrations. Like the wise householder in Matthew's Gospel, the church musician must be one "who can produce from his store both the new and the old."

77. The Church in the United States today needs the services of many qualified musicians as song leaders, organists, instrumentalists, cantors, choir directors, and composers. We have been blessed with many generous musicians who have given years of service even with meager financial compensation. In order that the art may grow and face the challenges of today and tomorrow every diocese and parish should establish policies for hiring and paying living wages to competent musicians. Full-time musicians employed by the Church ought to be on the same salary scale as teachers with similar qualifications and workloads.[39]

78. Likewise, in order that composers and publishers receive just compensation for their work, those engaged in parish music programs and those responsible for budgets must often be reminded that it is illegal and immoral to reproduce by any means either text or music of copyrighted materials without written permission of the copyright owner. The fact that these duplicated materials are not for sale but for private use does not alter the legal or moral situation of the practice.[40]

VI. MUSIC IN SACRAMENTAL CELEBRATIONS

79. While music has traditionally been part of the celebration of weddings, funerals and confirmation, the communal celebration of baptism, anointing and penance is only recently restored. The renewed rituals, following the Constitution on the Sacred Liturgy, provide for and encourage communal celebrations, which according to the capabilities of the congregation, should involve song.[41]

80. The rite of baptism is best begun by an entrance song;[42] the liturgy of the word is enhanced by a sung psalm and/or alleluia. Where the processions to and from the place of the liturgy of the word and the baptistry take some time, they should be accompanied by music. Above all, the acclamations—the affirmation of faith by the people, the acclamation immediately after the baptism, the acclamation upon completion of the rite—should be sung by the whole congregation.

81. Whenever rites like the anointing of the sick or the sacrament of penance are celebrated communally, music is important. The general structure is introductory rite, liturgy of the word, sacrament and dismissal. The introductory rite and liturgy of the word follow the pattern of the Mass. At the time of the sacrament an acclamation or song by all the people is desirable.

82. Confirmation and marriage are most often celebrated within a Mass. The norms given above pertain. Great care should be taken, especially at marriages, that all the people are involved at the important moments of the celebration, that the same general principles of planning worship and judging music are employed as at other liturgies, and above all, that the liturgy is a prayer for all present, not a theatrical production.

83. Music becomes particularly important in the new burial rites.[43] Without it the themes of hope and resurrection are very difficult to express. The entrance song, the acclamations, and the song of farewell or commendation are of primary importance for the whole congregation. The choral and instrumental music should fit the paschal mystery theme.

VII. CONCLUSION

84. We find today a vital interest in the Mass as prayer and here lies the principle of synthesis. When everyone with one accord strives to make the Mass a prayer, a sharing and celebration of Faith, then there will be unity—many styles of music, a broad choice of instruments, a wide variety of forms of celebration, but a single purpose: that men of faith may proclaim and share that faith in prayer and that Christ may grow among us.

Notes

1. Second Vatican Council, Constitution on the Liturgy (=CSL), No. 34.
2. Congregation of Rites, Instruction on Music in the Liturgy, March 5, 1967, No. 5e; *Roman Missal,* General Instruction (=GI), No. 73.
3. GI No. 313.
4. Bishops' Committee on the Liturgy (=BCL), April 18, 1966.
5. Congregation for Divine Worship (=CDW), Instruction on Mass for Special Gatherings, May 15, 1969.
6. BCL, February 17, 1967.
7. GI No. 1; cf. CSL No. 102.
8. Instruction on Music in the Liturgy, No. 11.
9. *Ibid.,* No. 8.
10. Cf. CSL, No. 112.
11. Cf. CSL, No. 114.
12. BCL, April 18, 1966.
13. National Conference of Catholic Bishops (=NCCB), November, 1967.
14. CSL, No. 121.
15. CSL, No. 28.
16. Instruction on Music in the Liturgy, No. 21.
17. BCL, April 18, 1966.
18. CSL, No. 114.
19. BCL, April 18, 1966.
20. Cf. CSL, No. 120; Instruction on Music in the Liturgy, Nos. 63-65; CDW Third Instruction, September 5, 1970, No. 3c.
21. NCCB, November 1967; cf. CSL No. 120.
22. GI, No. 8.
23. GI, No. 24.
24. Cf. *Roman Missal,* Blessing and Sprinkling of Holy Water, No. 1.
25. *Liturgy of the Hours,* General Instruction, Nos. 93-98.

26. GI, No. 54.
27. GI, No. 56.
28. GI, No. 57.
29. GI, No. 19, cf. Instruction on Music in the Liturgy, Nos. 28 and 36.
30. GI, No. 39.
31. GI, No. 56.
32. NCCB, November 1969.
33. *Ibid.*
34. NCCB, November 1968; cf. GI, No. 6.
35. Cf. GI, No. 30.
36. GI, No. 31.
37. GI, No. 43.
38. NCCB, November 1967.
39. BCL, April 18, 1966.
40. BCL, April 1969.
41. Cf. CSL, No. 27.
42. Rite of Baptism for Children, No. 5: 32 and 35.
43. Rite of Funerals, Introduction, No. 4.